Hassan by James Elroy Flecker

THE STORY OF HASSAN OF BAGDAD & HOW HE CAME TO MAKE THE GOLDEN JOURNEY TO SAMARKAND

A play in five acts

James Elroy Flecker was born on 5th November 1884, in Lewisham, London.

Flecker does not seem to have enjoyed academic study and achieved only a Third-Class Honours in Greats in 1906. This did not set him up for a job in either government service or the academic world.

After some frustrating forays at school teaching he attempted to join the Levant Consular Service and entered Cambridge to study for two years. After a poor first year he pushed forward in the second and achieved First-Class honours. His reward was a posting to Constantinople at the British consulate.

However, Flecker's poetry career was making better progress and he was beginning to garner praise for his poems including The Bridge of Fire. Unfortunately, he was also showing the first symptoms of contracting tuberculosis. Bouts of ill health were to now alternate with periods of physical well-being woven with mental euphoria and creativity.

Before his early death he managed to complete several volumes of poetry, which he continually revised, together with some prose works and plays. It was a small canon of work but on his death on 3rd January 1915, of tuberculosis, in Davos, Switzerland he was described as "unquestionably the greatest premature loss that English literature has suffered since the death of Keats".

Index of Contents
Characters
THE STORY OF HASSAN OF BAGDAD
ACT I
Scene I
Scene II
ACT II
Scene I
Scene II
ACT III
Scene I
Scene II
Scene III
ACT IV
Scene I
Scene II
ACT V
Scene I
Scene II

An Essay on James Elroy Flecker by JC Squire
James Elroy Flecker – A Short Biography
James Elroy Flecker – A Concise Bibliography

CHARACTERS
HASSAN, a Confectioner
The CALIPH HAROUN AR RASCHID
ISHAK, his Minstrel
JAFAR, his Vizier
MASRUR, his Executioner
RAFI, King of the Beggars
SELIM, a friend of Hassan's
THE CAPTAIN OF THE MILITARY
THE CHIEF OF THE POLICE
ALI   }
ABDU } Nondescripts
ALDER WILLOW }
JUNIPER   } Slaves
TAMARISK   }
THE PORTER of Yasmin's House
THE CHINESE PHILOSOPHER
A DERVISH
THE FOUNTAIN GHOST
A HERALD
THE PRISON GUARDS
PERVANEH
YASMIN
An AMBASSADOR, a WRESTLER, a CALLIGRAPHIST, a JESTER, GHOSTS, MUTES, DANCING WOMEN, BEGGARS, SOLDIERS, POLICE, ATTENDANTS and CASUAL LOITERERS

THE STORY OF HASSAN OF BAGDAD

ACT I

SCENE I

A room "behind the shop" in Old Bagdad. In the background a large caldron steaming, for the shop is a sweet-stuff shop and the sugar is boiling. The room has little furniture beyond the carpet, old but unexpectedly choice, and some Persian hangings (geometrical designs, with crude animals and some verses from the Koran hand-printed on linen). A ramshackle wooden partition in one corner shuts off from a living room what appears to be the shop.

Squatting on the carpet—facing each other:

HASSAN, the Confectioner, 45, rotund, moustache, turban, greasy grey dress.

SELIM, his friend, young, vulgarly handsome, gaudily clothed.

HASSAN [Rocking on his mat]
Eywallah, Eywallah!

SELIM
Thirty-seven times have you made the same remark, O father of repetition.

HASSAN [More dolefully than ever]
Eywallah, Eywallah!

SELIM
Have you caught fever? Is your chest narrow, or your belly thunderous?

HASSAN [With a ponderous sigh]
Eywallah!

SELIM
Is that the merchant of sweetmeats, that sour face? O poisoner of children, surely it would be better to cut the knot of reluctance and uncord the casket of explanation. And the poet Antari has justly remarked:

Divide your sorrow and impart your grief, O fool.
That good man comforteth beyond belief, O fool.

HASSAN [Inclining towards the mat]
None is good, save God.
And Abou Awas has excellently sung:

The importunate
Are seldom fortunate.

Nevertheless, know, Selim, that I am in love.

SELIM
In love! Then why sit moaning on the mat? Are there not beauties at the barbers, and lights of love at the bazaar?

HASSAN [Angrily]
Hold your tongue, Selim, or leave me. I was in earnest when I said I loved, and your coarseness is ill-fitting to my mood. And well I know I am Hassan, the Confectioner, yet I can love as sincerely as Mejnun; for assuredly she of whom my heart is bent is not less fair than Leila.

SELIM [Ironically]

Alas! I mistook the particular for the general, and did not recognise the purity of your intentions. But I would not mention Mejnun. Mejnun was young, and you are old, and he was a prince, and you are a Confectioner, and he was beautiful, and you are not, and he was very thin because of his sorrow, and you are fatter than those four-legged I mention not—God curse their herdsmen!

HASSAN
And if it be as you say, Selim, if I am indeed a fat, old, ugly tradesman, have I not good reason to be sorry and rock upon my mat, for how shall maintain my heart's desire?

SELIM
Listen to me, Hassan, why is it that in this last year you have become different from the Hassan that was Hassan? From time to time you talk strangely in your cups, like a mad poet; and you have bought a lute and a carpet too fine for your house. And now I feel you are losing your senses when I hear this talk of love from one who is past the age of folly.

HASSAN
It may be so, young man. Indeed, a think I am a fool.
It is the affliction of Allah.

SELIM
Tell me, at least, who she is. It may be she is not so unattainable as you imagine, unless indeed you have set eyes on the Caliph's daughter, or on the Queen of all the Jinn.

HASSAN
Listen, Selim, and I will tell you my affair. Three days ago a woman came here to buy loukoum of me, dressed as a widow, and bade me follow her to her door with a parcel. Alas, Selim! I could see her eyes beneath her veil, and they were like the twin fountains in the Caliph's garden; and her lips beneath her veil were like roses hidden in moss, and her waist was flexible as a palm-tree swaying in the wind, and her hips were large and heavy and round, like water melons in the season of water melons. I glanced at her but she would not smile, and I sighed but she would not glance, and the door of her house shut fast against me, like the gate of paradise against an infidel.
Eywallah!

[Recommences moaning.

SELIM
And where was the house of this widow who bought sweetmeats and had none to sell?

HASSAN
In the street of Felicity, by the fountain of the Two Pigeons.

SELIM [Musing]
It must be the widow of that Achmet they hung last year by the Basra Gate.

HASSAN
Which Achmet?

SELIM

The hairy one.

HASSAN
Istagfurallah! He fluttered like a bird. May I never soar so high.

SELIM
Istagfurallah! May I see you! I should burst with laughter and vultures with repletion. But tell me, you who have fallen so deeply in love, do you rejoice in your misfortune like a dervish in his dirt, or do you honestly desire satisfaction?

HASSAN
I desire satisfaction Selim. But I pray you talk no more of this.

SELIM
Well, take courage, faint heart, since all things can be cured save perversity in asses. Perhaps I can cure you of love.

HASSAN
By the Prophet, Selim, do not cure my love, cure her indifference.

SELIM [With sudden alertness]
There is only one way of doing that.

HASSAN
Which way?

SELIM
Do you believe in magic, Hassan?

HASSAN
Men who think themselves wise believe nothing till the proof.
Men who are wise believe anything till the disproof.

SELIM
What do we know if magic be a lie or not? But since it is certain that only magic can avail you, you may as well put it to the test. You can buy a philtre that can draw her love, and send her a jar of magic sweets.

HASSAN
I am ready to all things, ingenious Selim; but do you know a good magician?

SELIM
Zachariah, the Jew, has but lately arrived from Aleppo: he is the talk of all the market place, and a wonderful man if tales be true.

HASSAN
Have you the tales?

SELIM
I have this among many. They say that in Bokhara a man called him an offensive Jew and flung a stone at his head: and he caused the stone to be suspended in the air and the man too, so that the man walked all round Bokhara over the heads of the passers-by, who were astonished, and was constrained to enter his house by the upper window.

HASSAN [Incredulous]
Mashallah!

SELIM
And stranger than that. At Ispahan men say he took off the dome of the Great Mosque and turned it round and had a bath in it, and put it back again.

HASSAN
Mashallah!

SELIM
And strangest of all, at Cairo, for the amusement of the Sultan, he turned the whole population into apes for half an hour.

HASSAN
A very trifling change if you knew the Egyptians. I don't believe a word of all these tales. Yet, doubtless he is as good enough physician to make a love philtre. But are philtres any good?

SELIM
There can be no doubt that there are philtres which drive women to love, though their hearts be as strong and their heads as cold as the mountains of Qaf. But as for this Zachariah, I know he sells philtres at ten dinars the bottle: his shop is crowded with rich old women.

HASSAN
Eywallah, Salim, I am sick of love; but no damsel is worth ten dinars. And sages have remarked, "the ideal is expensive!" And philosophers have observed, "There are a thousand figs on the fig-tree and all as like as like."

SELIM
What! All the smooth, shining hills and well-wooded valleys in that country of love...All going for ten dinars!... And this is the man whose love is like Mejnun's! What is ten dinars to a man in love? You gave thrice that sum for this carpet.

HASSAN
A carpet is a carpet, and a woman is is a woman. It is not only the ten dinars. But you know that in this market I have a character. "Hassan", men say, "is a safe man. Hassan will not leave his jacket on the wall, or buy peas without prodding the sack." But if they hear: "A stranger came to Bagdad and no Mussulman and said he would do this, and Hassan has paid him ten dinars and got no gain", they will nudge each other when I walk abroad at evening, and say: "A sad end"; and another "Look at him, Saadet, my son, and drink no wine"; and another, "God preserve me from the friends of such a one!" and they will call out to me as they pass, "Ya Hassan, give me ten dinars that I may build a mosque!" and I will be shamed where I was honoured, and abased where I was exalted....

[A loud knocking on the floor of the adjacent shop causes **HASSAN** to retire thither hurriedly. As he disappears **YASMIN** peeps inquisitively, unveiled, through the little window in the partition.

SELIM
What an impudent little beauty.... Why, she had a widow's scarf on. She must be the princess! [Rocks with laughter) The unattainable ideal! And I have her address. It requires a frenzied lover to pay cash for a flask of coloured water. But I doubt if Hassan's sweets mingled with coloured water will do aught but can make her sick. Whereas a cake stuffed with those very dinars.... Allah, the dinars would not choke her! O thou fool Hassan!

Tell not thy shirt who smiled and answered "Yes":
Dream not her name, nor fancy her address.

[Enter **HASSAN**, pale and staggering.

HASSAN
Selim, in the name of friendship, take these ten dinars and buy me that philtre, and return with speed.

SELIM [Feigning irritation]
Allah! Am I your messenger?
Go yourself to the Jew.

HASSAN
I must prepare the sweetmeats this very hour, to send them to her before sunset. In the name of friendship, Selim, take the dinars and purchase me that philtre.

SELIM [Rising and taking dinars]
Do not make me chargeable, O Hassan, if the philtre is without effect. I only repeat what I have heard.

HASSAN
No, I will not blame you. But go quickly for the magic that nothing may be left unsampled that may prove beneficial.

[Exit **SELIM**; **HASSAN** makes up the fire and prepares his caldron, saying meanwhile.

That young man weareth out my carpet apace. I begin to think also he doth fray the braid of my affection. But if he buys me a good philtre I will forgive him. Oh, cruel destiny, thou hast made me a common man with a common trade. My friends are fellows from the market, and all my worthless family is dead. Had I been rich, ah me! how deep had been my delight in matters of the soul, in poetry and music and pictures, and companions who do not jeer and grin, and above all, and in the colours of rich carpets and expensive silks. But be content, O artist: thou hast one carpet; be content, O confectioner: thou hast one love—one love, but unattained...yet hadst thou been rich, O confectioner, never hadst thou found her.

Now I will make her sweets, such sweets, ah me! as never I made in my life before. I will make her sweets like globes of crystal, like cubes of jade, like polygons of ruby. I will make her sweets like flowers.

Great red roses, passionate carnations, raying daisies, violets, and curly hyacinths. I will perfume my roses (may they melt sweetly in her lips) with the perfume of roses, so that she shall say "a rose"! and smell before she tastes. And in the heart of each flower I will distil one drop of the magic of love. Did I not say "they shall be flowers"?

SCENE II

Moonlight. The Street of Felicity by the Fountain of the Two Pigeons. A house with a balcony on either side of the street. In front of one of the houses, **HASSAN**, cloaked: a **PORTER**.

HASSAN
Has she received the box, O guardian of the door of separation?

PORTER
From my hands, O dispenser of bounty.

HASSAN
What did thy mistress say?

PORTER
Sir, the hands of mediation are empty.

HASSAN [Giving a dinar]
I have filled them.
What honey dropped from that golden mouth?

PORTER
She said—may thy servant find grace—"Curses on that fat sugar cook and his love-sick eyes. Allah be praised, his confectionery is better than his countenance!"

HASSAN [Aside]
If she likes the confectionery, all may be well.
And what didst thou reply?

PORTER
I said: "His sweets sparkle like diamonds and rubies in the crown of OUR Caliph, and his sugar is as pure as his intentions." And she answered—the protection on thy slave—"his intentions may be pure, but his coat is greasy."

HASSAN
And did she eat the confectionery?

PORTER
I do not know. But within the hour I removed the box, and it was empty.

HASSAN

Ah! Salaam and thanks.

PORTER
And to thee the Salaam.

HASSAN
But tell me what is the name of thy mistress?

PORTER
Yasmin is her name, Sir.

HASSAN
A sweet name for a moonlight night. Salaam aleikum.

PORTER
Ya Hawaja, v'aleikum assalam!

[The **PORTER** returns and shuts the gate.

HASSAN [To himself]
What if the Jews are an older race than we and know old forgotten secrets? Alas, I believe no more in these Israelitish sweets. Could those drops of purple liquid command the spirit of love? And yet, who can say? the young men of the market-place laugh at all enchantments—but do they know how to spin the sun? On a night like this, does not the very fountain sing in tune and enchant the dropping stones? Ah, Yasmin?

[Taking a lute from beneath his cloak and a tuning it.

Yasmin...Yasmin...Yasmin...Yasmin.

[Intones to the accompaniment of the lute.

How splendid in the morning glows the lily; with what grace he throws
His supplication to the rose: do roses nod the head, Yasmin?
But when the silver dove descends I find the little flower of friends,
Whose very name that sweetly ends, I say when I have said, Yasmin.
The morning light is clear and cold; I dare not in that light behold
A whiter light, a deeper gold, a glory too far shed, Yasmin.
But when the deep red eye of day is level with for the lone highway,
And some to Mecca turn to pray, and I toward thy bed, Yasmin,
Or when the wind beneath the moon is drifting like a soul aswoon,
And harping planets talk love's tune with milky wings outspread, Yasmin,
Shower down thy love, O burning bright! for one night or the other night
Will come the Gardener in white, and gathered flower are dead, Yasmin!

[As **HASSAN** intones the last "Yasmin" with passion the shutters open, and **YASMIN**, veiled, looks out.

YASMIN

Alas, Minstrel, Yasmin is my name also, but it was for a fairer
Yasmin than me, I fear, you have strung these pearls.

HASSAN
There is no Yasmin but Yasmin, and you are Yasmin.

YASMIN
Can this be Hassan, the Confectioner?

HASSAN
I am Hassan, and I am a confectioner.

YASMIN
Mashallah, Hassan, your words are sweeter than your sweets.

HASSAN
Gracious lady, your eyes look down through your veil like angels through a cloud. Dare I ask to see your face, O bright perfection?

YASMIN [Roguishly]
Do you take me for a Christian, father of impertinence?
And since when do the daughters of Islam unveil before strangers?

HASSAN
It is said: he who speaks to the heart is no stranger.

YASMIN [Unveiling her eyes]
Are you satisfied, O importunate!

HASSAN
Never, till I have seen perfection to perfection.

YASMIN
You would shrivel, my poet. What about "the glory too far shed, Yasmin"?

HASSAN
Let me see you unveiled, Yasmin.

YASMIN
Anything to close the portal of your face.

[Unveiling.

There. Do I please thee, my Sultan?

HASSAN [Rapturously]
Oh, you are beautiful!

YASMIN
Prince of poets, is that all you have to say! Not a stanza, not a trope, not a turn, not a twist, not even a hint that the heavens are opened, or that there are two moons in the sky together?

HASSAN
There is but one.

YASMIN
Well confectioned, my confectioner! And now, Good-night.

HASSAN
O stay, Yasmin, you are too beautiful, and I too bold. I am nothing, and you are the Queen of the Stars of Night. But the thought of you is twisted in the strings of my heart; I burn with love of you, Yasmin. Put me to the proof, my lady; there was nothing I could not do for your bright eyes. I would cross the salt desert and wrest a cup of the water of life from the Jinn that guards it; I would walk to the barriers of the world and steal the roc's egg from its diamond nest. I would swim the seven oceans, and cross the five islands to rob Solomon ben Dawud of his ring in the palace where he lies sleeping in the silence and majesty of uncorrupting death. And I would slip the ring on your finger and make you mistress of the spirits of the air—but would you love me? Could you love me, do you love me, Yasmin?

YASMIN
There is love and love and love.

HASSAN [Passionately]
Oh, answer me!

YASMIN
I think I have been enchanted, Hassan; how, I cannot tell. Till this afternoon the thought of your appearance made my heart narrow with disgust. But since I ate your present of comfits—and they were admirable comfits, and I ate them with speed—my heart is changed and inclined toward you, I know not why or how, except it be through magic.

HASSAN [Aside]
She is mine, and magic rules the world!
[Aloud] Yasmin, shall I possess you, O Yasmin?

YASMIN
Am I not the desert waiting for the rain? Was I not born for passion, Hassan? Is not my bosom burning for kisses? Were not these arms made smooth and hard to fight the battle of love?

HASSAN
Are not your lips love's roses, your cheeks love's lilies, your eyes love's hyacinths?

YASMIN
Ya, Hassan, and my hair the net of love, and my girdle the chain of love that breaks at a lovers touch?

HASSAN
I am drowning in a wave of madness. Let me in, Yasmin; let me in!

YASMIN
Ah, if I could!

HASSAN
Why not?

YASMIN
Ah, if I dared!

HASSAN
What do you fear? It is night, and the street is silent.

YASMIN:
Ah, dear Hassan, but I am not alone.

HASSAN [Whispering]
Not alone? Who is there? Your mother?

YASMIN
No! One who you sent here.

HASSAN
I sent no one.

YASMIN
One of your friends.

HASSAN
A man?

SELIM [Poking his head out of the window]
Ya, Hassan, Salaam aleikum.
I thank you for directing my steps to this rose-strewn bower.

HASSAN [Astonished]
Selim!

SELIM
Thy servant always.

HASSAN [Wildly]
Selim!

SELIM
Be advised, O Hassan, go and seek the enchanted egg.

HASSAN

Selim, what do you here?

SELIM
Plunge not the finger of enquiry into the pie of impertinence, O my uncle.

HASSAN
Since when have I become your uncle, Selim, and how did I cease to be your friend?

SELIM
Since when did you aspire to poetry, O Hassan?
But I have heard these lines:

As from the eagle flies the dove
So friendship from the claw of love.

HASSAN
Love. What love do you mean, scum of the market?

SELIM
This.

[Puts a hand on **YASMIN's** shoulder.

HASSAN
May God strike thee blind, Selim, and shut the door of his compassion against thee!

SELIM
What is my crime, Uncle? How have I sinned against thee, or merited the solemn imprecation?

HASSAN
Do not touch her, you dog, do not touch her!

SELIM
Is it a crime to touch Yasmin, my Uncle? Am I not to be excused?
Is not her neck a pillar of the marble of Yoonistan?

[Puts his arm around her neck.

HASSAN
Torment of death!

YASMIN
Are not my arms like swords of steel, hard and cold, and thirsty for blood?

[Putting her arms around the neck of **SELIM**.

HASSAN
Fire of hell!

SELIM
Are not her eyes two sapphires in two pools?

HASSAN
Woe is me! Woe is me!

YASMIN
Are not my lips two rubies drenched in blood?

[Kisses him.

HASSAN
God, I shall fall!

SELIM [His face in **YASMIN**'s bosom]
Couldst thou but see, O my Uncle, the silver hills with their pomegranate groves; or the deep fountain in the swelling plain, or the Ethiopian who waters the roses in the garden, or the great lamp between the columns where the incense of love is burned. How can I thank thee, O my Uncle, for the name and address, and half the old Jew's dinars!

YASMIN
How can I thank thee, O my Uncle, for sending me this strong and straight young friend of thine to console my loneliness and desolation? Ah, it is bitter to be a widow and so young!

HASSAN [Putting up his hands to his head]
The fountain, the fountain!
O my head, my head!

YASMIN
Be not too rash, my Uncle, or thy hair will come away in thy hands.

HASSAN
If I could but reach your necks with a knife, children of Sheitan!

YASMIN
I was the sun of his existence, and now I am a child of Sheitan—and why? Never again will I trust the love of a man. I was a glory too far shed, and now he wants to open my neck. And already he has tried to poison me. Ya, Hassan, if you desire my death, send me some more enchanted sweets!

SELIM
Beware, O Hassan, of jesting with the Jinn.

YASMIN
Buy, O Hassan, no more juice from Jews.

SELIM

Much, I fear, O my friend, for thy character in the market. No more will men say: "Hassan is a safe man"; but they will nudge each other and say, "Beware of Hassan, Hassan is a great magician; he has talked with the spirit's of the air! Deal not with Hassan, O my son, Saadet, for he sells enchanted sweets that drive the consumer to madness. And at night Hassan becomes a cat, and walketh on the roofs after the female cats. Allah preserve me from the evil eye of such a one!" And another will say, tapping his forehead, "Speak no harm of poor Hassan, for his brain is very sick!" And the small, guileless boys will say, "Behold Hassan, who gave ten dinars for a pint of indigo and water."

HASSAN
Ah, death!

YASMIN
Look at him! He is drifting like a soul aswoon!
Go home, old fellow!

SELIM
Go home and write poems!

YASMIN
Go home, and cook sweets!

HASSAN
Yasmin! Yasmin! My head!

YASMIN
Begone, or I will cool thy head, thou wearisome old fool!

HASSAN
Yasmin! Yasmin!

[Stands with his arms outstretched.

YASMIN
Take this, my bulbul, to quench thy aspiration.

[Pours a jug of water over him, and slams the shutters to. **HASSAN** does not budge from his position.

HASSAN
O thou villainous, unclean dog, Selim. O thou unutterable woman. I will have you both whipped through the city and impaled in the market-place, and your bodies flung to rot on a dung-heap. O, my head aches! Ah, you foul swine! May you scream in hell for ever. O, my head—my head. For ever. Thou and thy magic and thy Jew. There is blood dripping from the wall.

[Banging on the gate.

I will break the house in. I will kill you. Ya Allah, I am splitting in twain. It is my own fault for having dreams and believing magic. Ya Allah, I am dying. Oh, Yasmin, so beautiful, so brutal. O burning bright; you have killed me! Farewell, and the Salaam!

[Falls under the shadow of the fountain. Silence. A light appears in the next house. Soft music starts; the first light of dawn shines in the sky.

[Enter the **CALIPH HAROUN AR RASCHID**, **JAFAR**, his Vizier, **MASRUR** (a Negro), his Executioner, and **ISHAK**, a young man, his poet, all attired as Merchants.

CALIPH
Ishak, my heart is heavy and still the night drags on, and still we wander in the crooked streets, and still we find no entertainment, and still the white moon shines.

ISHAK
O Caliph of Islam, is there not vast entertainment for the wise in the shining of the moon, in the dripping of that fountain, and in the shape of that tall cypress that has leapt the wall to shoot her arrow at the stars?

[The music which had stopped recommences.

CALIPH
But I hear music, and see lights. Come on, come on, we will snatch profit from this cursed night even yet, my friends, even at the eleventh hour.

JAFAR
Master, the night is far advanced, and you have not slept.
It is a late hour to seek for entertainment.

CALIPH
Jafar you are as prudent as a shopkeeper.

ISHAK
There lies his merit, Haroun! For he keeps the great shop of state, he sells the revenue of provinces, and buys in the lives of men.

CALIPH
Enough, enough. Call to them, Jafar, and see if they will let us in.

JAFAR
Oh, gentlefolk, in the name of Allah!

VOICE [From window, the person invisible]
Who calls?

JAFAR
Sir, we are four merchants who came yesterday night from Basra, and on our arrival we met in the street a man of Basra settled in Bagdad, who prayed us to dine with him. So we accepted and stayed late talking the talk of Basra, and left him but an hour ago. And since we were strangers to the city, we lost our way, and have been wandering ever since in search of our Khan and have not found it. And now

a happy chance has taken us to this street; for seeing lights and hearing music, indeed, sir, we hope to taste the cup of thy kindness, being men of honour, good companions and true believers.

VOICE
Then you are not of Bagdad?

JAFAR
No, sir, but of Basra.

VOICE
Had you been a Baghdad, you should not have entered for all the gold in the Caliph's coffers.

CALIPH
Then we may enter, being of Basra?

VOICE
If you enter, you will be in my power. And if you annoy me, I will punish you with death. But no one constraineth you to enter. Go in peace, O men of Basra.

CALIPH [Aside]
A rare adventure. [Aloud] We take the risk of annoying you,
O host of terror, and are now looking for the door.

VOICE
Since when did a door of good reputation open on to this street, my masters? Our door is far from here, and you are strangers and merry, and will not find it. But I will contrive a means for your ascent.

CALIPH
Jafar, I never suspected there was a great house in this poor quarter of the town. For from the outside it is a house like any other, except that it has no door; but inside, if this is but the back of it, it is of great extent and holds some secret. We shall make a discovery tonight, O Jafar.

JAFAR
Master, we have been warned of danger!

[A basket comes down.

CALIPH
Danger? What care I?

[Sits in the basket, and is drawn up.

JAFAR
Eh, Masrur, I could sleep a little.

MASRUR
You would wake in paradise if the Caliph heard you, Jafar.

[**MASRUR** waves his sword dexterously near **JAFAR's** neck.

JAFAR [As he ascends into the basket, pointing to **MASUR's** sword]
The path to Paradise is narrow and shiny, O Masrur.

MASRUR [With the grim motion of the sword]
Ya, Jafar, it is a short cut.

[**JAFAR** having ascended, **MASRUR** ascends, and the basket is let down for Ishak.

ISHAK [Alone]
Go on thy way without me, Commander of the Faithful. I will follow you no further. Find one more adventure if you will. For me the break of day is adventure enough—and water splashing in the fountain. Find out, Haroun, the secret of the lights and of the music, of a house that has no door, and a master that will admit no citizen. Drag out the mystery of a man's love or loss, then break your oath and publish his tale to all Bagdad, then fling him gold, and fling him gold, and dream you have made a friend! Those bags of gold you fling, O my generous master, to a mistress for night, to a poet for a jest, to a rich friend for entertainment, to a beggar for a whim, are they not the revenues of cities, wrung by torture from the poor? But the sighs of your people, Haroun, do not so much as stir the leaves in your palace garden!

And I—I have taken your gold, I, Ishak, who was born on the mountains free of the woods and winds. I have made my home in your palace, and almost forgot it was a prison. And for you I have strung glittering, fulsome verses, a hundred rhyming to one rhyme, ingeniously woven, my disgrace as a poet, my dishonour as a man. And I have forgotten that there are men who dig and sow, and a hut on the hills where I was born.

[Perceives **HASSAN**.

Ah, there is a body, here in the shade. Corpses of the poor are very common on the streets these days. They die of poison or the knife, but most of hunger. Mashallah, but you have not died of hunger, my friend, and there is that on your face that I do not like to see. By his clothes this was a common man, a grocer or a baker, his person ill-proportioned and unseemly, but by his forehead not quite a common man. I think—

JAFAR [From above]
Ishak, are you coming up?

ISHAK [Shouting back]
Wait a minute, I will come.

[To himself] What has curved his mouth into that bitter line?
He is an ugly man, but I maintain there is grace in his countenance.

What? A lute? Take my hand, O brother. You loved music too, and you could sing the songs of the people, which are better than mine—the songs I learnt from the mother of my mother.

[Taking the broken lute mechanically.

What was that one?

"The Green Boy came from over the mountains,
Joy of the morning, joy of his heart"?

I have forgotten it, and the lute is broken. Or that other:

"Come to the wells, the desert wells!
The caravan is marching down; I hear the camel bells."

[Resumes **HASSAN**'s hand.

Ah, brother, your hand is warm and your heart beating, you are not dead.

[Bathing **HASSAN**'s forehead with water from the fountain.

I shall know after all what has twisted your mouth awry.

CALIPH
Ishak, Ishak, we wait and wait.

ISHAK
May I not be free one hour, to breathe the dawn alone! Ah!...

[Takes **HASSAN**'s body and drags it to the basket.

I come, my master!

[Puts **HASSAN** in the basket.

There, take my place, brother, and find your destiny. I will be free to-night, free for one dawn upon the hills!

[As **HASSAN** is drawn up in the basket, **ISHAK** walks rapidly away.

ACT II

SCENE I

A great room. To the left three arches lead out onto the balcony where the personages **CALIPH**, **JAFAR** and **HOST** are collected. The interior of the room is blazing with lights, but empty. The architecture of the room is curious on account of the wide, low arches which cut off a square in the centre. The furniture of the room is in rich, rather vulgar Oriental taste.

CALIPH

Ishak, Ishak, we are waiting and waiting.

JAFAR
Ishak! Ishak! Perhaps he is faint.

CALIPH
Faint!

JAFAR
Let me go down and see what he is doing. I think I hear him talking.

CALIPH
He is talking to shadows. He has one of his evil fits tonight. Do not trouble your head or mine about him. He presumes on our friendship, and forgets the respect due to us. Am I to be kept waiting like a Jew in a court of justice, I the Master...

JAFAR [Quickly]
We are not in Basra, Sir. But see, the rope has tightened.
[To **MASRUR**]
Haul, thou whose soul is white.

RAFI [Helping with ropes to **CALIPH** who stands idle]
God restore to you the use of your arms, my brother from Basra.

[**HASSAN** rolls out of the basket, filthy and the inanimate.

Yallah, Yallah, on what dunghill did this fowl die?
Is this your man of honour?

JAFAR [Astonished]
Host of the house, this is not our companion, and we have never set eyes on him before.

RAFI
Then what is this?

CALIPH
Our friend has played a trick on us—may Allah separate him from salvation!—and sent up this body in place of himself. Come let us tip it out into the street.

RAFI [Feeling **HASSAN**'S pulse]
Wait; this man is by no means dead, and the mill of his heart still grinds the flour of life.
Ho, Alder!

[Enter **ALDER**, a young and pretty page.

ALDER
At his master's service.

RAFI
Ho, Willow!

WILLOW [Younger still]
At his lord's order.

RAFI
Juniper!

JUNIPER
At his Pasha's command.

RAFI
Tamarisk!

TAMARISK [A little boy a with a squeaky voice]
At his Sublimity's feet.

CALIPH [Aside to **JAFAR**]
Truly, this is charming: an illustrious example of decorum and good taste.

RAFI
Transform this into a man, my slaves. Revive him, bathe, soap, scent, comb him, clothe him with a ceremonial coat and bring him back to us.

ALDER
We hear,

WILLOW
We honour,

JUNIPER
We tremble,

TAMARISK
—and obey.

CALIPH [Entering the great room of the house]
Thy house is of grand proportions and eccentric architecture, my Host; it is astonishing that such a house should look out on to so mean a street.

RAFI
It is an old house where the Manichees (the devil roast all heretics!) once held their meetings before they were all flayed alive. It is called the house of the moving walls.

CALIPH
Why such a name?

RAFI
I do not know at all.

CALIPH
The merry noise of music that we heard is silent.

RAFI
I waited for your permission, my guests, before continuing my meagre entertainment. Ho, music! Ho, dancers!

[Claps his hands.

[Music plays. The **HOST** enters the room and motions his **GUESTS** to be seated in silence.

CALIPH
Verily, after this prelude, and in this splendid palace, we shall see dancing women worthy of Paradise.

JAFAR
God grant it, Master.

CALIPH [To **JAFAR**]
Hush, I hear the pattering of feet.
The wine of anticipation is dancing through my veins.
O Jafar, what incomparable houris will charm our eyes to-night?
What rosy breasts, what silver shoulders, what shapely legs, what jasmine arms!

[In good order, marching to the music, there enter the most awful selection of Eastern **BEGGARS** the eye could imagine, or the tongue describe. They are headed by their **CHIEF**, a rather fine fellow, in indescribable tatters. He leads the **CHORUS** with a song, half intoned in the Oriental style.

Fathers of two feet, advance,
Dot and go ones, hop along,
Two feet missing need not dance,
But will join us in the song.

CHORUS OF CULS-DE-JATTE
But will join you in the song.

Show your most revolting scar;
People never weary of it.
The more nauseous you are—
More the pity and your profit.

CHORUS
And your profit, profit, profit.

Cracked of lip and gapped of tooth,
Apoplectic, maim or mad,

Blind of one eye, blind of both,
Up, the beggars of Bagdad.

CHORUS
Up, the beggars of Baghdad.

There is a cellar, I am told,
Where a little lamp is lit,
And that cellar's full of gold,
Sacks and sacks and sacks of it.

CHORUS [Hoarsely]
Sacks and sacks and sacks of it,
Stacks and stacks and stacks of it.
Open eyes and stiffen backs,
There are sacks and sacks and sacks;
And gold for him who lacks of it.

[The **HOST** lifts his hand. The **BEGGARS** all fall flat on their faces. Dance music.

[Enter right, a **BAND** of fair, left, a **BAND** of dusky beauties.

THE DANCING GIRLS
Daughters of delight, advance,
Petals, petals, drift along;
Cypress, tremble! Firefly, dance!
Nightingale, your song, your song!

THE FAIR
We are pale

THE DARK
—as dawn, with roses,
O the roses, O desire!
We are dark,

THE FAIR [Curtsying]
but as the twilight
Shooting all the sky with fire.

CHORUS
Daughters of delight, advance,
Petals, petals, drift along,
Cypress, tremble! Firefly, dance!
Nightingale, your song, your song!

[They surround the **BEGGARS**, dancing, and point at them.

LEADER OF THE FAIR
From what base tavern, of what street
Were dragged these dogs, that foul our feet?

LEADER OF THE DARK
O sisters, fly, we shall be hurt:

[The **LEADER OF THE BEGGARS** catches her.

Leave go my ankle, son of dirt.

LEADER OF THE BEGGARS
Lady, if the dirt should gleam,
Feel, but do not show surprise:
Things that happen here would seem

[Rises to his feet, his rags drop off, and he shines in gold.

Paradox in Paradise.

[The infirmities and rags of the whole **BAND** disappear as if by magic, as they rise and shout in **CHORUS**.

CHORUS
Paradox in Paradise

[**RAFI** raises his hand. **ALL** stand at attention.

VOICES
Hush, the King speaks.
The King of the Beggars.
The King.

LEADER OF THE BEGGARS
The King of the Beggars, the Caliph of the Faithless. The Peacock of the Silver Path, the Master of Bagdad!

[The **BALLET** line the room behind the arches.

JAFAR [Aside, astonished]
King of the Beggars?

MASRUR [Aside, astonished]
Master of Bagdad?

CALIPH [Aside, astonished]
Caliph of the Faithless? Allah kerim, this is a jest indeed!

RAFI [Throwing off his outer garment and discovering himself superbly dressed in a golden armour]
Subjects and guests. Now that the night before our day is ending, and the Wolf's Tail is already brushing the eastern sky; now that our plot is ready, our conspiracy established, our victory imminent, what is there left for me to tell you, O faithful band? Shall I say, be brave? You are lions. Be cunning? You are serpents. Be bloody? You are wolves.

See now, Bagdad is still in dreams that in a few minutes shall be full of fire, and that fire redder than the dawn. You have begged—you shall buy: you have fawned—you shall fight: you have plotted—you shall plunder: you have cringed: you shall kill.

How loud they snore, those swine whose nostrils we shall slit to-day! Copper they flung to us, and steel we shall give them back; good steel of Damascus, that digs a narrow hole and deep.

But as for the Peacock of Peacocks, that sack of debauch, that Caliph, alive in his coffin, I and none other will nail him down, with his eyes staring into mine. His gardens, fountains, summer houses, and palaces; his horses, mules, camels, and elephants, his statues of Yoonistan, and his wines of Ferangistan, his eunuchs of Egypt, and his carpets of Bokhara, and his great sealed boxes bursting with unbeaten gold, and his beads of amethyst, and his bracelets of sapphire, all this and all his women, his chosen flower-like women, are yours for lust and loot and lechery, my children—all save her of whom I warned you—a woman who was mine, and who shall sit unveiled with me on the throne of all the Caliphs... and when you see us sitting on that throne together, then you shall cry...

THE BEGGARS [Taking up with a shout]
The Caliph is dead! The Caliphate is over!
Long live the King!

JAFAR [In indignation]
These words are not holy, even in jest.

RAFI
O guests of an hour, I pray you put the tongue of discretion into the cheek of propriety.

JAFAR
Propriety! The host's obligations are greater than the guests.
It is not good taste to speak thus before the invited.
We pray you only that we may withdraw at once.

RAFI
Then who will withdraw me, my masters, from the vengeance of the Caliph, once you have talked a talk with the Captain of his Guard?

JAFAR
We give you our promise: we are men of honour.

RAFI
If you were thieves, as we are, I might trust you. But, if, as you say, you are men of honour, honour will drive you panting to the Caliph's gate, and honour will swiftly break a promise made to a this and a rebel, under compulsion.

JAFAR
Sir, I pray you, no more of this, be it jest or earnest.
It will soon be morning: we must away: we have pressing business: our clients await us.

RAFI
And give me their names, O my guests, and tonight I will fling their gold and their carcasses together at your feet.

JAFAR
We insist that you let us go.

RAFI
O merchants, tell me but this one thing: Do you dwell in fine houses in the port of Basra?

JAFAR
We have no mean abodes.

RAFI
Are your apartment spacious and well furnished?

JAFAR
Well enough.

RAFI
Then tell me further, have you soft carpets on the floors of those rooms?

JAFAR
There are carpets.

RAFI
Great, rich, soft carpets from Persia and Afghanistan?

JAFAR
Yes.

RAFI
It is a pity. Soft carpets make soft the sole of the foot.
And they who have soft feet should ever keep them on the road of meekness.

MASRUR [Drawing his sword]
Dost thou dare threaten us, bismillah!

RAFI
Truly, O most disgusting negro, comprehension and thou have been separated since your youth. Shall I then drop needle of insinuation and pick up the club of statement? Shall I tell you three guests of mine, with the plainness of plainness and the openness of plainness, that if you offer one threat more,

propose one evasion more, or ask one question more, I will thrash your lives head downwards from your feet.

[Enter **HASSAN** finely dressed, and ushered in by the **FOUR BOYS** through the rows of **DANCERS**.

HASSAN [Lamenting]
Eywallah, eywallah, eywah, eywah, Mashallah! Istagfurallah!

RAFI
Why, here is the fourth guest!

ALDER
We have washed him: he needed it.

WILLOW
Combed him: it was necessary.

JUNIPER
Scented him: it was our duty.

TAMARISK
Clothed him: it was our delight.

HASSAN [As before]
Eywallah! Yallah Akbar! Y'allah kerim! Istagfurallah!
Eywallah! Hassan is ended! Hassan is no more! He is dead!
He is buried! He is a bone! Y'allah kerim!

RAFI
Eyyah Hassan, if that is your name, have my boys not treated you well?
If they have hurt you with their tricks, by the Great Name, I will...

HASSAN
I pray you, I pray you. Thrash no one's life out downwards from their feet, O master, and above all, not mine.

RAFI
Ah, you heard me! Take courage. All that I require of my guests, good Hassan, is genteel behaviour.

HASSAN
Ah! Who are all these terrible men?

RAFI
Beggars of Bagdad! Ten thousand more await my signal on the streets. In a few minutes they will surprise the drowsy Palace Guards, sack Bagdad, kill the Caliph and make me King.

HASSAN [Stupefied]
What has become of me this night! Just now I was in Hell, with all the fountains raining fire and blood.

RAFI
Come, Hassan, you are only just in time; the cold dawn which ends the revellers' dark day will soon be uncurtaining the blue. One bowl to pledge me victory, O guests, for I must away and win it, and you shall lie here to sleep away the destruction of Bagdad. At least you shall say this of your host—he gave us splendid wine.

[The **FOUR SLAVES** hand round the bowl; the **CALIPH** refuses.

[To **CALIPH**) Sir, you do not drink.

CALIPH
I obey the Prophet.

RAFI
What wine do they grow in the desert of Meccah, or on the sandhills of Medina? Ah, had the Prophet tasted wine of Syria or the islands, the book would have been shorter by that uncomfortable verse.

JAFAR
Come, host! I at all events will pledge you. There is ever fellowship between those who have drunk wine together, be they murderers or thieves or Christians.

MASRUR
Host, on the day when I shall spill your blood, I shall drink a little in remembrance of this bowl of wine. Till then your health!

[Drinks.

RAFI [Sarcastically]
Ye are three jolly fellows of amiable disposition.

[Drinks.

I thank you, negro, I drink to yours.

HASSAN
I drink to forget a woman, but will this little cup suffice?

RAFI
Nor ten, nor ten thousand little cups like these, if you have loved. Tonight I shall fill my bowl of the oblivion with the blood of the Caliph of Bagdad. Brother, will that great cup suffice?

HASSAN [In terror]
Call me not brother, thou savage man, who dost talk of shedding the holiest blood in Islam!

RAFI

When high office is polluted, when the holy is unholy, when justice is a lie, when the people are starved, and the great fools of the world are in high office, then dares a man talk of shedding the holiest blood in Islam?

CALIPH
Also when one has a vengeance to wreak on the Caliph and a claim on a lady of his household.

MASRUR
Why do you want to nail him in his coffin alive? Tell us the tale.

JAFAR
Tell us, if would not have us think you a mad man or a buffoon.

CALIPH
Tell us about the woman; what harm can do you since we are in your power?

RAFI [After hesitation]
Yes, what harm can it do, if for my own sake, to relieve the heaviness of my heart, I tell you something of my story?

My name is Rafi. I come from the hills beyond Mosul, where the men walk free and the women go unveiled. There I was betrothed to Pervaneh, a woman beautiful and wise. But the very day before our marriage the Governor of Mosul remembered my country and invaded it with a thousand men. And little enough plunder they got from our village, but they caught Pervaneh walking alone among the pine woods and carried her away. When I heard this I leapt on my horse and galloped to Mosul, prepared to slay the Governor and all the inhabitants thereof single-handed, if evil had come to Pervaneh. But there I found she had already been sent with a raft full of slaves down the Tigris to Bagdad. Whereupon I hired six men with shining muscles to row me there. We arrived at Bagdad at the end of the third night's rowing at the grey of dawn. I sprang out of the raft like a tiger, and ran like a madman through the streets, crying "The Slave Market! Tell me the way, O ye citizens! The Slave Market, O the Slave Market!"

And suddenly turning a corner I came upon the market, which was like a garden full of girls in splendid clothes grouped in groups like flowers in garden beds and some like lilies, naked. I ran around the market to find Pervaneh and all the women laughed at me aloud, and behold there she stood; she who had never worn a veil before, the only veiled woman in all the market, for she had sworn to bite off her lips if her master would not veil her: but I knew her by the beauty of her hands, and I cried: "O dealer, the veiled woman for a thousand dinars!" And the dealer laughed in the way of dealers at the presumption of my offer and demanded two thousand, and so I purchased for gold the blood of my own heart, and she lifted her veil and sang for joy and hung upon my neck, and all the slave girls clapped their hands.

But at that moment there entered into the market a negro eunuch, so tall and so disgusting that the sun was darkened and the birds whistled for terror in the trees. And all the dealers and the slaves bowed low before him. Coming to my dealer, he cried: "Why dost thou sell slaves before the Caliph has made his choice?"

Then turning to to Pervaneh, he said, "Go back to thy place."

And I cried, "She is my purchase." But the eunuch said,
"Hold thy peace; I take her for the Caliph."

And suddenly two guards seized Pervaneh, and I drawing my sword was about to hew the eunuch into a thousand pieces, Pervaneh made a sign to me, and looking up I saw I was surrounded by men at arms. And Pervaneh cried in the speech of my country, as they carried her way: "I will die, but I will not be defiled: rescue me alive or dead, soon or late, and avenge me on this Caliph, may the ravens eat his entrails!"

That is my story, and for this reason I will nail the Caliph down in his coffin, bound and living and with open eyes.

CALIPH [In horror]
Bound and living, with open eyes! Thou devil!

MASRUR
Is that all the story?

JAFAR
Will you tear up the Empire for the honour of a girl?

CALIPH [In fury]
And set your worthless passion in scale against the splendour of Islam!

RAFI
Is this Haroun the splendour of Islam? Is the prosperity of these people, a rosy slave in his serai, or their happiness, a fish in his silver fountain?

JAFAR
God will frustrate thee.

RAFI
If he will. Farewell, my guests. I go to avenge Pervaneh, and to wash Bagdad in blood.

JAFAR
And what of us?

RAFI
It is well be used that you are my guests, for you are rich and proud, and eminently deserve destruction. But you are safe in his room as in an iron cage; you will only hear, as in a dream, the crash of the fall of the statue of tyranny.

CALIPH [Rushing to intercept him]
By the thick smoke of Hell's Pit and the Ghouls that eat man's flesh, you shall not go, and we shall not stay.

RAFI
Look twice before you touch me!

[He leaps behind the archway. The **BEGGARS** and the **WOMEN** are now lined close to the wall of the room and the **GUESTS** are isolated in the centre. From behind every pillar appears an **ARCHER** with bow drawn taut directed on the startled **GUESTS**.

CHORUS OF BEGGARS AND DANCING GIRLS
Today the fools who catch a cold in summer
Will fly for winter in the windy moon.

To-day the little rills of shining water
Will catch the fire of morning oversoon.

To-day the state musicians and court poets
Will set new verses to a special tune.

Today Haroun, the much-detested Caliph
Will find his Caliphate inopportune.

RAFI [Silencing the **SINGERS** with a wave of his hand; to the **GUESTS**]
Did not someone ask me why this house was called the House of the Moving Walls?

CALIPH
I asked the question.

[Sheets of iron with a crash covering the apertures of the arches. The four **GUESTS** are completely walled in.

RAFI, BEGGARS AND WOMEN [From behind the iron partitions with a shout]
Answered!

JAFAR
This is a disastrous situation!

[The **BEGGARS** Tramp out to martial music.

VOICES OF THE BEGGARS [Retreating]
Today Haroun, the much-detested Caliph,
Will find Caliphate inopportune!

JAFAR [Listening at the wall]
They have all left the room.
At least we are alone. Let us shout, they may hear us from the street.

MASRUR [Banging on the wall]
Eyyah! Help, help, men of Bagdad!
The Caliph is in danger! The Caliph is in prison!...
Come up and save the Caliph, the Master of Men, the Shaker of the World!...

[Silence.

CALIPH
There comes no answering cheer...

JAFAR
I had forgotten the height of this room above the streets: and on either side stretches the empty garden of this house!

[The **CALIPH**, **JAFAR** and **MASRUR** rush around as though trying to find a way out of their prison, and banging on the iron walls. **HASSAN** takes his seat on the carpet.

CALIPH
Allah! and this room is a box within a box like a Chinese toy. And that man will surprise my soldiers in the chill of dawn, and sack my palace and burn Baghdad. He will discover my identity and bury me alive!

JAFAR
Alas, Master! What shall we do?

CALIPH
Thou dog! Thou dirt! Thou dunghill! Thou dustheap! Did I make thee Vizier to ask counsel or to give it? Find out what we shall do! Thou hast let me fall into a trap, and now dost quiver and quake and shiver and shake like a tub of whey on the back of a restive camel: my kingdom is reduced from twelve provinces to twelve square cubits: my subjects from thirty millions unto three, but Bismillah! one of my subjects is the Executioner, and Mashallah! another one merits execution: and Inshallah! if thy head doth not immediately devise a practical scheme of escape it shall dive off my shoulders and swim across the floor.

JAFAR
What shall happen, shall happen. But here is one who is occupied in meditation, and is aloof from the circumstances of the moment: let us invite him to Council.

CALIPH
Ho, thou Hassan! What occupies thy spirit?

HASSAN
I am examining the square of carpet. It is of cheap manufacturer, inferior dye and unpleasant pattern.

CALIPH
Art thou a carpet dealer?

HASSAN
No, sir, I am a confectioner,

CALIPH
And I am the Caliph.

HASSAN

As my heart surmised. O Commander of the Faithful!

[Performs the ceremonies prescribed.

CALIPH
Canst thou give me one gleam of hope of salvation, Hassan the Confectioner? If not, Masrur shall cut off all our heads, beginning with thine, I dare not fall into that man's hands alive.

HASSAN
But I dare! O spare me, spare me! What of the man who put me in the basket? He will know where we are, and come to our rescue.

CALIPH
No good—no good. I would rather depend on the mercy of Rafi than on the whim of Ishak. Masrur, unsheathe. There is no hope.

HASSAN
Thy pardon on thy servant: there is hope! Behold the light!

[Points to crack between bottom of the iron wall and floor, towards the balcony.

CALIPH
By the seven lakes of Hell, we are not mice!

HASSAN
A mouse could not pass. But what, O Master, of a message?

CALIPH
A message?

HASSAN
Written out black on paper, and dropped into the street.

CALIPH
Ho, Jafar, thou art a fool to this man! Take out thy pen and write.
Warn the Captain of the Soldiers. Warn the Police. Describe our position.
Offer the the Government of Three Provinces to the man who picks up the paper.
Write clearly, write quicker. Time's flying.
Write, and we are saved. Write for the Salvation of Bagdad;
Write for the safety of Islam! O Hassan, the Confectioner,
If we are rescued I will fill my mouth with gold!

[JAFAR having written on a long roll of paper, they thrust it in the crack.

HASSAN
No: at the corner here, where there is no balcony and the wall
drops straight into the street.

[**MASRUR** pokes out the paper with his sword.]

CALIPH
And now how shall we employ the time of waiting for our deliverance?

JAFAR
I shall meditate upon the mutability of human affairs.

MASRUR
And I shall sharpen my sword upon my thigh.

HASSAN
And I shall study the reasons of the excessive ugliness of the pattern of this carpet.

CALIPH
Hassan, I will join thee: thou art a man of taste.

SCENE II

[See ACT I, last Scene]

Again, the street outside the house—the Street of the Fountain, with the balcony of **RAFI** and the balcony of **YASMIN** opposite. Cold light before dawn.

[On the steps of the Fountain, two tired **MENDICANTS** asleep. One slowly rubs his eyes and looks round him. A paper comes floating down. One tired **MAN** lazily catches it.

FIRST LOITERER
Here comes a new chapter of the Koran falling down from heaven.

SECOND LOITERER
Is it written, Abdu?

ABDU
It is written, Ali.

ALI
Read what is written, Abdu.

ABDU
I cannot read. Am I schoolmaster?

[Folds paper, puts it in his belt, and prepares to sleep again. Several interesting **ORIENTALS** pass by.

ALI
Abdu!

ABDU
I sleep.

ALI
I can read: give me the paper.

ABDU
I am asleep: get up and take it from my belt if you want it,
Ya Ali, I am heavy with a great sleep, like a tortoise in November.

ALI
Ya Abdu, I am too languishing to move. It is a paper and it is written.
It does not matter. To-morrow or the next day it will be read.

ABDU
To-morrow or the next day I shall wake and pass it to you.

[Interval: more interesting **ORIENTALS** go by.

ALI [With sudden inspiration]
Blow me the paper, Abdu.

ABDU
Alas, Allah sent thee to trouble the world!

[**ABDU** blows the paper over. **ALI** with infinite difficulty spells it out, murmuring:

ALI
Ha, alif, alif, re wow wow 'ain jeem—ah, ye blessed ones in Paradise, is it thus ye write a jeem? Nun—but art thou a nun, O letter, or a drunkard's qaf? Verily an ape has written this with his tail: I have the second line. [With a start] Ho, Abdu, whence came this? Do not pretend to sleep. Answer me.

ABDU
From the sky: how do I know?

ALI
Let me look at the sky.

[Rolls on his back and stares upward.

I tell you, Abdu, a mighty joker has flung this from the balcony.

ABDU
Allah plague him and his pen and thee! Is there no peace in the world?

ALI

Here it is written, and do thou listen, O Abdu, for this is the strangest of the strange writings that are strange: "Whoever findeth this paper, know that the Caliph is in the house above, a prisoner, and his friends prisoners, and in the extremity of danger, he and they, with all Bagdad. Let the rescue be swift and sudden, but above all secret. The iron walls must be lifted from beneath. And send a man at once to the Guard, O fortunate discoverer, to warn them to protect the palace against the Beggars of Bagdad, and thou shalt be made Governor of Three Provinces.
Signed,
Jafar, the Vizier."
[Bursting into laughter] Three Provinces, well I know their Three Provinces! Some rich young reveller hopes to play a game with poor old Ali, even as a game was played on the son of Abdullah, whom they dressed as a woman and placed in the Grand Vizier's Harem, and his reward came hailing down on his toes. [In a lower voice.] And I tell you, Abdu, what if the Caliph were in the house and his friends? What if this were true? Who would believe me? Who am I to rescue the Caliph? I never meddle in politics.

ABDU
May the great gripes settle on thee and on the Caliph and the mother of the Caliph. Shall I not sleep? And now there comes a disturbance down the road. Ya, Jehannum, the Police!

[CHIEF OF POLICE with ISHAK.

ISHAK
I tell you, I do not know precisely where I left them. It was somewhere in this quarter. It may have been this balcony they went to or that, but there are a thousand balconies. It was above a fountain, but there are a million fountains. I tell you they always come back. Have you not already twenty such scares as these for the safety of the Caliph?

CHIEF OF POLICE
Never and on no preceding occasion has his exalted name been so long delayed in his return to the palace. The day is dawning.

ISHAK
I tell you, if you do find him you will get no thanks, O man of arms. Will you dare to unstick the Ruler of the Moslem World from the embrace of his latest slave girl or dash the cup of pleasure from his reluctant hand?

CHIEF OF POLICE
I tell you, if you do not find him, man of letters, I will have you impaled upon a monstrous pen.

[Seizes him.

ISHAK
Thou beastly, blood-drinking brute and bloated bully, take off thy stable-reeking hands.

CHIEF OF POLICE
Yallah, these poets. They talk in rhyme.

ALI [Who has risen and salaamed, advancing]
I pray you, Sirs,...

CHIEF OF POLICE
O thou maggot! Darest thou address us?

ALI
I pray you only regard...

CHIEF OF POLICE
I pray you only remove, or I will split you from the top.

ISHAK
Do you not see that he has a paper, and that his manners are superior to yours, O Captain of Police? Let me look at thy paper....Ah—ah. Whence came this, O virtuous wanderer?

ALI
From that balcony, may thy slaves be forgiven!

CHIEF OF POLICE
This is a very important clue. Let us break in the door.

ISHAK
There is no door. But first of all send word to the Palace Guard.

CHIEF OF POLICE [To a **SOLDIER**]
Ali

[To the other **ALI**, who runs and says: Excellence, I hear and obey.

Not thou, fool. Did Allah make the name Ali for thee alone?
Who art thou that I should address thee? Are there not ten thousand Alis in Bagdad, and wilt thou lift up thy head, O worm, when I say Ali?
[To **POLICEMAN**]
Here is my ring. Take this paper, and run with all thy might and show it to the Captain of the Palace Guard.

POLICEMAN
I hear and obey.

[Starts off.

ISHAK [Stopping him]
Wait!

CHIEF OF POLICE
What right have you to stop my man, you bastard son of a quill-bearing barn-fowl?

ISHAK

Since when had a bludgeoning policeman the practical good sense of a thought-breathing poet? Tell them, Ali, to send a few men with levers and ladders.

CHIEF OF POLICE
It is well ordered: run, run, Ali!

ISHAK
You other Ali, who brought the paper...

ALI
Master?

ISHAK
How long is it since any paper was thrown from the balcony?

ALI
How do I know time? The time to go to market and buy a melon.

CHIEF OF POLICE
By the great pit of torment, this swine-faced has had the paper a good hour! By the red blaze of damnation, thou maggot, why didst thou not run with this at once to the Palace Guard?

ALI
I had a great fear, and I thought it was a jest.

CHIEF OF POLICE
A jest! Rivers of blood, a jest!
The life of the Caliph of Bagdad, a jest?
The safety of the Empire a jest!
I knew thee a traitor from thy face.
I will teach thee jesting. I will teach thee fear.
Ho, Mahmud, Zia, Rustem, down with his head and up with his heels.

ALI [As his feet are looped into the pole to receive the bastinado]
Ya, Abdu, you had the letter first, it is yours. Will you not claim it and the reward. Alas, that the Governor of Three Provinces should be treated thus!

ABDU
Do I meddle in politics? Hit him hard, O Executioner, for he is a great disturber of peaceful citizens. But as for me, O Ali, lest my sleep be troubled by thy groaning, I will make my way a little further on.

[Exit.

[The **EXECUTIONERS** proceed with their work, but stop on entrance of **CAPTAIN OF THE MILITARY** with **SOLDIERS**.

[On the balcony opposite house where **CALIPH** is imprisoned appears **YASMIN**.

YASMIN
Look, look, Selim! there's a man being beaten.

SELIM
Come in quick! this is a riot or some trouble; come in quick, and shut the shutters fast.

YASMIN
You are a valiant protection indeed for frail-as-a-rose ladies in danger's hour.

[They remain at window.

CAPTAIN OF MILITARY [To **CHIEF OF POLICE**]
Sir.

CHIEF OF POLICE
Sir.

CAPTAIN OF MILITARY [Saluting]
Captain of the Victorious Army, at your service.

CHIEF OF POLICE [Saluting]
Chief of the August Police, at yours.

CAPTAIN OF MILITARY [Bowing]
I am honoured.

CHIEF OF POLICE [Bowing]
I am overwhelmed.

ISHAK
Come, Sirs, brush away, I implore you, the cobwebs of ceremony with the broom of expedition.

CHIEF OF POLICE
Sir, when men of action meet, the place of the man of letters is inside his pencase.

CAPTAIN OF MILITARY
A moment! Ere we proceed, Chief of Police, may I ask why this man is undergoing punishment?

CHIEF OF POLICE
Since your excellency deigns to enquire, for urgent reasons of police.

CAPTAIN OF MILITARY
They must have been very urgent indeed before you would permit such an inopportune disturbance outside the very house where our Lord the Caliph is imprisoned. You have seriously impaired our chances of a speedy and effective rescue.

CHIEF OF POLICE [Drawing his sword and whirling it about]

Thou melon head, thou, thou dung pig, thou brother of disaster, get thee hence with thy knock-kneed band of fatherless brigands, ere I have thee arrested for unnatural crime.

CAPTAIN OF MILITARY
Out with thy sword, thou big-bellied snatcher up of burglars, thou manacler of little boys, thou terror of the peaceful market, I will teach thee to insult the slaughterers of the infidel host.

ISHAK [Interrupting the **COMBATANTS**]
Is this a time for indecent brawling?
Quick, where are the ladders?

A SOLDIER [Pompously]
In the rear, Sir, in the rear.

[The ladders are brought along.

CHIEF OF POLICE [To **POLICEMAN**]
Place a ladder.

CAPTAIN OF MILITARY [To **SOLDIERS**]
Place a ladder.

[Each goes up his ladder at the same time: bang at wall and are answered: shout for levers which are procured, and assistance which speedily arrives. The iron wall is lifted up, and **CALIPH** and the REST disclosed seated peaceably awaiting their deliverance, the lamp still burning.

CHIEF OF POLICE
My royal master!

CAPTAIN OF MILITARY
August Lord.

CHIEF AND CAPTAIN [Together]
I have saved thee, Master.

[Each attempts to seize the **CALIPH**.

CHIEF OF POLICE
Honourable Police!...

CAPTAIN OF MILITARY
Honourable Military!...

CHIEF OF POLICE
It has been the high privilege of this grovelling slave to rescue the Lamp of the World! I shall carry him down.

CAPTAIN OF MILITARY

Permit me to observe, O fire-spitting Battle Cleaver, that I was the first up this ladder, and though I tremble to obscure the Sun's Brilliance with my dirty little hand, yet it is I who have the prior claim.

[**MASRUR** pushes them aside, and assists the **CALIPH** down the ladder. **JAFAR** and **HASSAN** follow. Shouts of "Long live the Caliph" from all the people gathered in the street. The **SOLDIERS** salute. The **CALIPH** raises his hand. Silence.

CALIPH
Is my Palace safe?

MASRUR
O Lord and Master, we pray so.

CALIPH
And my people?

JAFAR
Around thee, O Lord and Master.

YASMIN [From her balcony]
By the Prophet, here is Hassan with the Caliph!

CALIPH
Are we all saved?

MASRUR
All, by the providence of Allah.

JAFAR
And the wisdom of Hassan.

CALIPH
And the Guard warned?

CAPTAIN OF MILITARY
All warned and at their posts, my Lord.

CALIPH
Allah, deliver our enemies into their hands. Let Hassan come to me.

HASSAN [Prostrating himself]
Master!

CALIPH [Raising him]
Rise, Hassan. This Hassan, yesterday a stranger, has to-night by his skill and invention, saved my life and rescued this city from a greater peril than my death.

CROWD

May it be far!

CALIPH
Therefore here and now, in the presence of all, I nominate Hassan to my court, to hold rank among my subjects second to none save to Jafar, my Grand Vizier.

YASMIN [Who has been at her balcony with **SELIM**]
O Allah!

CROWD
Honour to Hassan. Honour to Hassan.

HASSAN
Master, I sold confectionary in the market.

JAFAR
Thou shalt now confection the sweets of prosperity.

ISHAK [To **HASSAN**]
Why, Hassan. You are the man with the broken lute.

CALIPH
Is that the voice of Ishak?

ISHAK
It is the voice of Ishak that has often sung to you.

CALIPH
Why did you abandon me, Ishak, and flee into the night? I do not know I shall forgive you.

ISHAK
I was weary of you, Haroun-ar-Raschid.

CALIPH
And if I weary of you?

ISHAK
You will one day or another, and you will have me slain.

CALIPH
And what of this day that dawns?

ISHAK
Dawn is the hour when most men die.

CALIPH
Your death is granted you, Ishak; you have but to kneel.

[A red glow on the horizon.

ISHAK [As he kneels calmly]
Why have they pinned the carpet of execution on the sky?

MASRUR
It is the Caliph's dawn.

JAFAR
Thy dawn, O Master!

ISHAK
Thy dawn, O Master of the world, thy dawn;
The hour the lilies open on the lawn,
The hour the grey wings pass beyond the mountains,
The hour of silence, when we hear the fountains,
The hour that dreams are brighter and winds colder,
The hour that young love wakes on a white shoulder,
O Master of the world, the Persian Dawn.

That hour, O Master, shall be bright for thee:
Thy merchants chase the morning down the sea,
The braves who fight thy war unsheathe the sabre,
The slaves who work thy mines are lashed to labour,
For thee the waggons of the world are drawn—
The ebony of night, the red of dawn!

CALIPH
Sheathe thy sword, Masrur! Would you kill my friend?

MASRUR
I hear and obey.

CALIPH
I must go swiftly to my palace. But to you, Ishak, I leave the care of this man you sent up to me in the basket, who proved the salvation of Bagdad. Teach him the ceremonies and regulations. Is my chair ready?

MASRUR
Ready, Lord and Master.

[Exit **CALIPH** in chair, and **JAFAR** and **CROWD**. **ISHAK** signs to those who would kiss **HASSAN**'s feet to leave him.

YASMIN [On balcony opposite. Giving **SELIM** a great clout on the ear]
Go, leave my sight, you fool. I shall burst with fury.
You made me insult Hassan, and now he is going to court.

SELIM [Astonished]
Eh, Yasmin, Yasmin how could I know?

ISHAK
Ah, bismillah, I had not forgotten you, O man with the broken lute.

HASSAN
The broken lute? The broken lute?

ISHAK
Here you were lying, at this fountain, like one dead.

HASSAN
Was it here? Is that the balcony? Who are you? What do you know?

ISHAK
Quietly, friend, quietly, your head is weak with joy.

HASSAN
With joy? Do I know what is true or false? Do I know if the Caliph is the Caliph? And if the Caliph is the Caliph may he not mock me too? What is joy? Let me look at that balcony for joy. I dare not look, I fear she is there. Ah, it is she.

[**YASMIN** takes the rose from her hair and flings it at **HASSAN**, then retires within.

ISHAK
Are you fortunate in love as well as in life, O Hassan? But come away.
This conduct ill beseems a minister of state; you are not unobserved.

HASSAN
I am coming. The rose is poisoned.

ISHAK
O friend, is this talk for the ardent lover?

HASSAN
Are you my friend? You, Ishak, the glorious singer of Islam?
And if you are my friend, are you like those who were my friends before?

ISHAK
Last night, I found you lying like a filthy corpse beneath this window, but I knew by your lute and your countenance that you were a poet, like myself, and I was sorry to think you dead.

HASSAN
A poet? I? I am a confectioner.

ISHAK

You are my friend, Hassan.

HASSAN
Then consider this rose. This rose is more bitter than colocynth. For, look you, friend, had she not flung this rose, I would have said she hated me and loved another; it is well. She had the right to hate and love. She could hate and she could love. But now, ah, tell me, you who seem to be my friend, are all you poets liars?

ISHAK
Ya, Hassan, but we tell excellent lies.

HASSAN
Why do you say that beauty has a meaning? Why do you not say that beauty is hollow as a drum? Why do you not say that it is sold?

ISHAK
All this disillusionment because a fair lady flung you a rose!

HASSAN
Last night I baked sugar and she flung me water: this morning I bake gold and she flings me a rose. Empty, empty, I tell you, friend, all the blue sky.

ISHAK
Come, forget her and come away. I will instruct you in the pleasures of the court.

HASSAN
Forget, forget? O rose of morning and O rose of evening, vainly for me shall you fade on domes of ebony or azure. This rose has faded, and this rose is bitter, and this rose is nothing but the world.

ACT III

SCENE I

The Garden of the **CALIPH**'s palace: in front of a pavilion. The **CALIPH**: **HASSAN** in fine raiment, a sword of honour at his side.

CALIPH
Yes, what the chief Eunuch told you is all true, my Hassan. Our late host, the King of the Beggars, was captured hiding in the gutter of his roof. This evening I shall judge him and his crew in full divan. And in the divan thou shalt appear, O Hassan, clothed in thy robe of ceremony, and seated on my right hand.

HASSAN
Alas, O Serene Splendour, thy servant is a man of humble origin and limited desires. I am one who would obey the old poet's behest:

Give all thy day to dreaming and all thy night to sleep:

Let not Ambition's Tyger devour Contentment's Sheep!

I am not one to open my mouth at divans, or to strut among courtiers in robes of state. Sir, excuse me from these things. Dispose thy favour like a high golden wall, and protect the life of your servant from the wind of complication. But at evening, when God flings roses through the sky, call me then to some calm pavilion, and let us hear Ishak play and let us hear Ishak sing, till you forget you are Lord of all the World, and I forget I am a base-born tradesman; till we discover the speech of things that have no life, and know what the clods of earth are saying to the roots of the garden trees.

CALIPH
Have no fear. You shall inhabit the place I shall assign you in untroubled peace, and meditate till your beard grows into the soil and you become wiser than Aflatun. But in this case you are a witness and must be present at my divan, be it but for this once only. And you shall call me Emir of the Faithful, Redresser of Wrong, the Shadow of God on Earth, and Peacock of the World. But in this garden you are Hassan, and I am your friend Haroun, and you must address me as a friend a friend.

HASSAN [Kissing the **CALIPH**'s hand]
O master, you speak gently, but I must fear you all the more.

CALIPH
But why? I am but a kindly man. I love single-heartedness in men as I love simplicity in my palace. There you have seen floors with but one carpet—but that carpet like a meadow. You have seen walls with but one curtain—but that curtain a sunset on the sea. You have seen white rooms all naked marble: but they await my courtiers, all dressed like flowers. If, therefore, I avoid complexity in the matter of walls and floors, shall I not be simple in the things of heart and soul? Shall I not, Hassan, be just your friend?

HASSAN
Master, I find thy friendship like thy palace, endowed with all the charm of beauty and the magic of surprise. As thou knowest, I am but a man of the streets of Bagdad, and there men say, "The Caliph's Palace, Mashallah! The walls are stiff with gold and the ceilings plated with silver, and the urinals thereof are lined with turquoise blue." And hearing men say this, many a time hath Hassan the Confectioner stroked the chin of Hassan the Confectioner saying, "O, Hassan, thy back parlour is less ugly than that, with its tub for boiling sugar, and its one good Bokhara carpet hanging on the wall. And twelve months did I work at the tub, boiling sugar to buy that carpet."

CALIPH
What a man you are for poetry and carpets! When you tread on a carpet, you drop your eyes to earth to catch the pattern and when you hear a poem, you raise your eyes to heaven to hear the tune. Whoever saw a confectioner like this? When did you learn poetry, Hassan of my heart?

HASSAN
In that great school, the Market of Bagdad. For thee, Master of the World, poetry is a princely diversion, but for us it was a deliverance from Hell. Allah made poetry a cheap thing to buy and a simple thing to understand. He gave men dreams by night that they might learn to dream by day. Men who work hard have special need of these dreams. All the town of Bagdad is passionate for poetry, O Master. Dost thou not know what great crowds gather to hear the epic of Antari sung in the streets at evening? I have seen cobblers weep and butchers bury their great faces in their hands!

CALIPH
By Eblis and the powers of Hell, should I not know this, and know that therein lies the secret of the strength of Islam? In poems and in tales alone shall live the eternal memory of this city when I am dust and thou art dust, when the Bedouin shall build his hut upon my garden and drive his plough beyond the ruins of my palace, and all Bagdad is broken to the ground. Ah, if there shall ever arise a nation whose people have forgotten poetry or whose poets have forgotten the people, though they send their ships around Taprobane and their armies across the hills of Hindustan, though their city be greater than Babylon of old, though they mine a league into earth or mount to the stars on wings—what of them?

HASSAN
They will be a dark patch upon the world.

CALIPH
Well said! By your luck you have saved the life of the Caliph,
O Hassan; but by your conversation you have won the friendship of Haroun.
Indeed—but at what are you gazing as if enchanted?

HASSAN
What a beautiful fountain, with the silver dolphin and the naked boy.

CALIPH
A Greek of Constantinople made it, who came travelling hither in the days of my father, the Caliph El Madhi (may earth be gentle to his body and Paradise refreshing to his soul!). He showed this fountain to my father, who was exceptionally pleased, and asked the Greek if he could make more as fine. "A hundred," replied the delighted infidel. Whereupon my father cried, "Impale the pig." Which having been done, this fountain remains the loveliest in the world.

HASSAN [With anguish]
O Fountain, dost thou never run with blood?

CALIPH
Why, what is the matter, Hassan?

HASSAN
You have told a tale of death and tyranny, O Master of the World.

CALIPH [In a sudden and towering rage]
Do you accuse my father of tyranny,
O fellow, for slaying a filthy Christian?

HASSAN [Prostrating himself]
I meant no offence. My life is at your feet.
But you bade me talk to you as a friend.

CALIPH
Not Ishak, not Ishak himself, who has been my friend for years, would dare address me thus.

[Bursting into laughter.

Rise, Hassan. Thy impudence has a monstrous beauty, like the hindquarters of an elephant.

HASSAN
Forgive me, forgive me.

CALIPH
I forgive you with all my heart, but, I advise you, speak in conformity with your character and of things you understand, and never leave the Garden of Art for the Palace of Action. Trouble not your head with the tyranny of Princes, or you may catch a cold therein from the Wind of Complication. Keep to your poetry and carpets, Hassan, and make no reference to politics, for which even the market of Bagdad is an insufficient school.

HASSAN [Dolefully]
I hear and obey.

CALIPH
Forget it now; set your mind on pleasant things. Have you noticed this little pavilion in front of which we have talked so long? This is your little house, good Hassan, where you shall find a shelter from the wind you so much dislike and all all other blasts that harm or chill.

HASSAN
My little house?

CALIPH
I chose it for you, knowing your disposition. Here in this remote corner of the garden you will hear no noise of street or Palace, but enjoy complete repose.

HASSAN [With rapture]
Mine, this little house? Mine, this sweet-scented door!

CALIPH
Knock on it and see.

[**HASSAN** knocks. A door opens and **ALDER**, **WILLOW**, **JUNIPER**, and **TAMARISK** appear. **TAMARISK** the youngest, has somewhat of a mouse's squeak.

ALDER [To **CALIPH** with prostration]
O, Emir of the Faithful!

WILLOW [To **CALIPH** with prostration]
O, Redresser of Wrong!

JUNIPER [To **CALIPH** with prostration]
O, Shadow of God on earth!

TAMARISK [To **CALIPH** with prostration]
O, Peacock of the World!

ALDER [To **HASSAN** with prostration]
Master!

WILLOW [To **HASSAN** with prostration]
Master!

JUNIPER [To **HASSAN** with prostration]
Master!

TAMARISK [To **HASSAN** with prostration]
Master!

[They stand, their hands in their sleeves, across the doorway.

HASSAN
But these are the slaves of the King of the Beggars, who bathed me, and anointed me, and brought back my soul into my eyes, whence a woman had all but driven it forever.

CALIPH
I have rescued them from the ruin of their master's house as their polite and finished manners deserve, and I have given them to you since you are likely to need and appreciate their service.

HASSAN
And so faces not altogether strange will welcome me to my home.

[Kneels and kisses **CALIPH's** hand.

CALIPH
Say not a word. For the pen of happiness hath written on thy face the ode of gratitude.
[To **SLAVES**]
Is all ready?

ALDER [Pompously]
Ready, O Gardener of the Vale of Islam.

WILLOW
Prepared, O Lion...

CALIPH
Enough! Conduct your master into his house, show him all there is inside, and serve him faithfully. Enter with them, Hassan; delicious has been our converse, but Jafar, the Vizier has been awaiting me some two hours.

[As **HASSAN** is about to prostrate himself.

No, it is thus Haroun takes leave of his friends.

[Kisses him on both cheeks. **HASSAN** watches till he is out of sight, pensive. Then he goes to the fountain and observes it a moment. Then advances slowly to the folding door of the pavilion which **ALDER** and **WILLOW** hold open for him.

ALDER
Fortunate be thy entry!

WILLOW
Prosperous thy sojourn!

JUNIPER
Quiet thy days!

TAMARISK
And riotous thy nights!

SCENE II

The private apartment within the pavilion. A bed. Fine furniture. A window with a view on the garden.

[Enter **HASSAN** followed by his **SLAVES**.

HASSAN
In that apartment, therefore, I shall receive guests.
But in this apartment, whom?

ALDER
Such ladies, Master, as you desire to honour.

HASSAN
Yes, yes. I must visit the market and see.

[Staring at the floor, with a start.

Wulluhi, what is that?

TAMARISK
The carpet, Master.

HASSAN
One of the wonderful new carpets of Ispahan.
A hunting scene. The Prince. His followers.
Leopards and stags and three tigers, and an elephant—his head only.
O amazing carpet.
And everywhere great scarlet flowers, very stiff and fine.
O exquisite carpet. I have never seen so bright as scarlet.

[With a sudden earnestness.

Tell me. You were his slaves...?

ALDER
Master?

HASSAN
Well, well, we will not talk of it. How clearly that fountain sounds outside with its little splash!

ALDER
I pray you, Master, the Caliph said you should particularly observe this mirror with the carven frame.

HASSAN [Looking at himself]
By the Prophet, what a Phoenix I have become!
Provided I do not stumble on my sword.

WILLOW
The Caliph hoped you should not fail to remark this exquisitely upholstered couch.

JUNIPER
The Caliph hopes you would admire these toilet requisites in alabaster.

TAMARISK
The Caliph hopes you will make good use of this very slender whip for our correction.

HASSAN
A whip? For your correction, O slaves of charm? Am I the man to spoil good almond paste with streaks of cochineal?

ALDER
Thou art pleased, O my Master?

HASSAN
Pleased? Look at the acacia tapping at my window; one night it will come in softly and fling its moonlit blossom at my feet. But this is no place for a man to live alone. Without a doubt I must visit the market. They have Circassians; I have always wanted a Circassian. She must be very young.... I have not finished the excellencies of the room. These three chests, what do they contain?

ALDER
This chest, O Master, contains your new robes. One of them is embroidered with red carnations and silver bells.

HASSAN
Was there ever generosity like this!

WILLOW

This chest, O master, contains curtains, hangings, and cushions for the sofa. One of the cushions is embellished with fifteen peacocks.

HASSAN
Fifteen peacocks! And all those peacocks dumb!

JUNIPER
This chest O master, contains fresh linen for your bed.
All marked with your name.

HASSAN
Marked with my name! And what have you to say, Tamarisk?

TAMARISK
That bed...

HASSAN
That bed is not a chest. But doubtless it also contains fresh linen marked with my name.

TAMARISK [Tremulous]
That bed contains a most beautiful lady.

HASSAN [Jumping]
What?

TAMARISK
A most beautiful lady. She said she must see you, and gave me ten dinars.

YASMIN [As **HASSAN** tears aside the curtains of the bed]
Hassan!

[She is dressed in a cloak and veiled.

HASSAN
What voice?

YASMIN
Hassan.

[She unveils.

HASSAN
Thou!

YASMIN
I came: I hid: I waited.

HASSAN

Why?

YASMIN
Why does a woman hide in the bed of a man?

HASSAN [Furiously]
You dared! Stay here, slaves.
Will you leave me at this moment, you fools who let this women in?
[To **YASMIN**]
You dared?

YASMIN
What is there a beautiful woman dare not dare?

HASSAN
But your impudence is vile. Out of it! Get you back to Selim.

YASMIN
I have left Selim.

HASSAN
Left Selim to come to me?

YASMIN
I found Selim a coward and a fool. I have discovered in you a man of taste and valour. How could I have known before? But what matter? Am I not white enough to follow the caravans of Wealth and Power?

[Flinging out her arms.

Is this for Selim or that for Selim?

HASSAN
Back to him, and no more words! You darken the world before my eyes.
If he is a fool and a coward, you're nothing but a whore.
Go, or my slaves shall fling you head foremost down my steps.

YASMIN
I have left Selim because he proved a coward, a fool, a poor man and a nobody. I have come to you because you are rich, famous, and a man of taste. The day you fall into disfavour (may it be far, O my Master!) I shall undoubtedly leave you. Till that day you will find me faithful. I am that which you call me—but I bring you a fair merchandise.

HASSAN
I thank you, O seller of yourself. I buy no tainted meat.
I beg you seek another market, and that extremely soon.

YASMIN [Rubbing her face and rising lightly]
I did not know I had a taint,

O Master. The mirror must deceive me.
But merchandise must be well inspected before its inferiority is assured.
It must be seen and touched. Will you see and will you touch?

HASSAN [Stepping back]
Oh, away, away! Why did you seek me out?
Is it to rain back my words upon my face?
Or do you hope once more to show me yourself limb after limb in the embrace of a new Selim? I pray you, however, spare the water from the jug. My fire needs no quenching.

YASMIN [Suppliant]
Be generous. It beseems the Caliph's friend to be generous.
If I have made you jealous, do I not not offer you a sumptuous revenge?

HASSAN
Rise, take your pardon, and depart. Shall I tell you again?
If you need money, the slaves will give it you at the door.

YASMIN
You are as cold as ice.

HASSAN
You are brazen.

YASMIN
I am brave. Farewell, I see you are not a man of love.

HASSAN
Farewell. And defile no more the word love with your painted lips.

YASMIN [Lingering at the door]
Yet there is a little of love's language that I do not know. When the bird of night sings on the bough of the tree that rustles outside your window, and the shadows creep away from the moon across the floor, I could have sung you a song sweeter than the nightingales and shown you a whiteness whiter than the moon.

HASSAN
Ah—go!

YASMIN
Because I was cruel could I not be kind? Because you can buy my body, can you buy my soul? Because I am of the people have I no songs to sing? Because I have sinned have I no secret to impart? Go to market, O Hassan, and buy your Circassian girl. And one day you shall say: Had Yasmin but lied to me of love, it were better than this fool's sincerity.

HASSAN
Ah, leave me!

YASMIN
There are lilies by the thousand in the meadows: there are roses by the thousand in the gardens, and all as like as like—but there is only one shape in the world like mine. There is only one face in the world where the eyebrows arch and the eyes flash—where the nostrils are set just so, and the lips are parted thus. There is no other arm beneath the skies that has has here this curve and here this dimple, and here the light soft golden hairs. There are rows and rows of young fair girls in the Caliph's harem and many as fair as I, but none whose veins are these veins, whose flesh is this flesh, fiery and cool, whose body swings like mine upon the heel.

[Flinging off her cloak.

Will you see and will you touch?

[Approaching.

Will you see and will you touch?

[Putting her arm round his neck.

Will you touch?

HASSAN [With a shout as he pushes her back]
Slaves, tear off this woman!

YASMIN [As the **SLAVES** force her back]
Eh, your slaves are violent!

HASSAN [To **SLAVES**]
Hold her!

YASMIN
But you must let me go.

HASSAN
I will not let you go.

YASMIN
Come, I see you are but a sour fellow, for whom pleasure is but vain.
I will take away the hateful. Let me pass.

[She attempts to escape.

HASSAN [To his **SLAVES**]
Hold her!

[**ALDER** and **WILLOW** each grip an arm. **JUNIPER** grips her ankles. She is held standing. Her cloak falls. She is clothed in short jacket and trousers of white silk with a pattern of blue flowers: her waist is naked, in the Persian style.

YASMIN
Ah—what will you do to me? You forgave me.

HASSAN [To **YASMIN**]
Ah, I forgave you the insults and all that hour of shame.
And Allah shall forgive you your trade if Allah wills.
But you have pressed your foul body on mine—you have breathed your poison on my cheek, and twined your snakes (God break them!) round my breast. Preparethen to die, for it is not right for the sake of mankind would you should walk any more upon the road of earth..

YASMIN [Quietly, but in terror]
To die! What do you mean! No, no!
Ah, murder, ah!

HASSAN
Do you hear the fountain dripping—drop by drop—drop by drop?
So shall your blood fall on my carpet and colour me more red flowers.

YASMIN [Recovering]
I am not afraid.

HASSAN
Do you expect mercy? I left mercy with my sweets.
For all these years I have been a humble man, of soft and kindly disposition—such a man as the world and a woman hate. But now I shall never again be the fool of my fellows. Now all Bagdad shall know and say: "We thought Hassan a mild man and a kind man; our children stole his sweets and he did but stroke his beard, while to a beggar he had known three days he would instantly lend three dinars. And behold, he has become powerful and hath cut down the body of Yasmin the infamous who had done him wrong, as a woodman cuts a tree. Yallah, our knees shall bend when Hassan goes driving by!" Yasmin, stiffen your sinews and close your eyes.

YASMIN
Not with the sword, not with the sword!

HASSAN
Let me taste the ecstasy of power. Let me drink of the fulness of life.
Let me be one of those who conquer because they do not care.

[He draws the sword: Yasmin cries out loud.

You are Yasmin, the poor, the beautiful, the proud: I am Hassan, rich and passionate and strong. You have hurt me, I will hurt you; it is the rule of the game, and the way of the world. Do I hate you? I do not know or care. Do I love you?—then love shall drive the blade in deep. You are the world's own stupendous harlot, and I will cut you clean in two.

[He swings sword over his head to strike.

YASMIN [With a shout at once of terror and triumph]
I will not close my eyes!
I will look at you. You dare not do it, looking at my eyes!

[**HASSAN** whirls sword round.

You dare not do it, looking at my eyes!

[**HASSAN** flings the sword across the room and falls across the divan, his face in his hands.

HASSAN
O Hassan the Confectioner, thou art nothing but an old man and a fool!

[**YASMIN** comes up to **HASSAN**. The **BOYS** silently disappear. He draws her toward him.

[With infinite tenderness.

Yasmin!

SCENE III

The Great Hall of the Palace. The room is plain, white marble. **ISHAK** alone, in his robes of Court Chamberlain.

[Enter **SOLDIERS** with the **CAPTAIN OF THE MILITARY** and the **CHIEF OF POLICE**.

[The **SOLDIERS** intone "The War Song of the Saracens.")

SOLDIERS [sing]
We are they who come faster than fate: we are they who ride early or late:
We storm at your ivory gate: Pale Kings of the sunset beware!
Not on silk nor on samet we lie, nor in curtained solemnity die
Among women who chatter and cry and children who mumble a prayer.
But we sleep by the ropes of the camp, and we rise with a shout and we tramp
With the sun or the moon for a lamp, and the spray of the wind in our hair.

From the lands where the elephant are to the forts of Merou and Balghar,
Our steel we have brought and our star to shine on the ruins of Rum.
We have marched from the Indies to Spain, and by God we will go there again;
We have stood on the shore of the plain where the Waters of Destiny boom.
A mart of destruction we made at Yalula where men were afraid,
For death was a difficult trade, and the sword was a broker of doom;
And the Spear was a Desert Physician, who cured not a few of ambition,
And drave not a few to perdition with medicine bitter and strong.

And the shield was a grief to the fool and as bright as a desolate pool,

And as straight as the rock of Stamboul when our cavalry thundered along:
For the coward was drowned with the brave when our battle sheered up like a wave,
And our dead to the desert we gave, and the glory to God in our song.

THE SOLDIERS [Cheering]
Allah Akbar! [etc.]

CHIEF OF POLICE
That is a splendid song your soldiers sing, O breaker of infidel bones.
Permit an inglorious policeman to inquire what flaming victory you celebrate today. Such is my loathly ignorance, I knew not the Caliph's army (may it be ever plosh in seas of hostile blood!) had even left Baghdad.

CAPTAIN OF MILITARY
It is true we have not left Baghdad, But perchance we have saved it from destruction. For when the Caliph's Police have allowed a conspiracy to ripen undetected, It is our duty to mow down the conspirators. It is true we did but vanquish beggars—but they were beggars to fight. Half of them we slew and one-half we captured, and, since the police believe no clue but the ocular, here they are. A victory is well worth a song.

CHIEF OF POLICE
Allah, such a song! I thought: "At the least they have captured Cairo."

CAPTAIN OF MILITARY
To save Bagdad is better than to capture Cairo.

CHIEF OF POLICE [Pointing to the captive **BEGGARS**]
Behold only the chain-mail of the vanquished!

CHIEF OF MILITARY
It is an old song, a glorious great battle song, and in mocking it thou has displayed on an absence of education, thou dragger of dead dogs from obscure gutters.

ISHAK
Is this talk for the high divan, Captain? Ye have saved Bagdad? Bagdad is no longer worth saving. You rose-petal-bellied parasites of the palace, how dare you sing that song?

CAPTAIN OF MILITARY
Allah, these poets talk in rhyme.

[Enter the **HERALD** announcing various personages, who enter as he announces them and are motioned to their place by **ISHAK**.

HERALD
Abu Said, Prince of Basra, to do homage. Fahraddin, Prince of Damascus, to do homage. Al Mustansir, Prince of Koniah, to do homage. Tahir Dhu'l Yaminayn, governor of Khorasan, to do homage.

The great calligraphist, Afiq of Diarbekir, master of the riqa and the shikasta hands: also of the Peacock style, and of painting in miniature.

ISHAK [Aside]
Episodes of considerable obscenity.

HERALD
The celebrated Turkoman wrestler, Yurghiz Khan, whose thighs are three cubits in circumference.

ISHAK [Aside]
As fat as a woman's, but not as nice.

HERALD
Abu Nouwas, the Caliph's jester. The Rajah of the Upper Ganges, come hither to do homage with a present of 800 bales of indigo.

ISHAK [Aside]
And never dyed his beard.

HERALD
Hang Wung, the wisest philosopher in China, come hither to study the excellence of the habits of true believers. He is a hundred and ten years old....

ISHAK [Aside]
And perfectly blind.

HERALD
Anastasius Johannes Georgius, ambassador of the infidel Empress Irene, mistress till God wills of Constaniniyeh and the lands of Rum, come here on a vain errand....

ISHAK
He understands no word, and believes we do honour to his name.
But the jest is thin, my Herald.

HERALD
Abul Asal, the wandering dervish, come hither to remind kings that they are but dust.

ISHAK
"Where lies Nushiravan the Just?"

DERVISH
The rhyme helps reason. In the dust.

ISHAK
The platitudes of dervishes do not much disturb the beatitudes of kings.

HERALD
Masrur, the Executioner, come hither to make several beggars the dusty equivalents of monarchs.

ISHAK
Ah, you may well shiver, poor captives: it is draughty among your rags.

HERALD
Hassan ben Hassan al Bagdadi, the Caliph's friend.

SOLDIERS
Long live Hassan and the shadow of Hassan and the friend of Hassan ben Hassan al Bagdadi!

ISHAK [Drawing **HASSAN** aside]
Come hither, friend of the Caliph; do not forget that you are the man with the broken lute.

HASSAN
What is a friend?

ISHAK
Are you not in favour? Has not the Caliph taught you?
You have a royal friend.

HASSAN
He is generous: he is gracious: he is intimate. He has leant on my arm, he has embraced me, he has called me by that name "friend". But I tremble before his eyes.

ISHAK
You have found out. No man can ever be his friend.

HASSAN
Alas, that is because he is exalted far above mankind!

ISHAK
Alas, no: but because he uses that supremacy to play the artist with the lives of men.

HASSAN
What do you mean, Ishak?

ISHAK
Have you not seen the designer of carpets, O Hassan of Bagdad, put here the blue and here the gold, here the orange here the green?
So have I seen the Caliph take the life of some helpless man—who was contented in his little house and garden, enjoying the blue of happy days—and colour his life with the purple of power, and streak it with the crimson of lust: then whelm it all with the gloom-greys of abasement, touched with the glaring reds of pain, and edge the whole with the black border of annihilation.

HASSAN
He has been so generous. Do not say he is a tyrant!
Do not say he delights in the agony of men!

ISHAK
Agony is a fine colour, and he delights therein as a painter in vermilion new brought from Kurdistan. But shall so great an artist not love contrast? To clasp a silver belt round the loins of a filthy beggar while a slave darkens the soles of his late vizier, is for him but a jest touched with a sense of the appropriate: and I have seen it enacted in this very room.

HASSAN
But you are his friend.

ISHAK
As you are. It is elegant for a monarch to condescend: it is refreshing for a monarch to talk as man to man. It is artistic for a monarch to enjoy the pleasures of contrast and escape the formalities of Court.... But here comes the preceder of the Caliph, the penultimate splendour of the divan, a man noble without passion, sagacious without inspiration, and weak as a miser's coffee.

HERALD
The Tulip of the Parterre of Government, the Shadow of the Cypress Tree, the Sun's Moon, Jafar the Barmecide.

SOLDIERS
Long live the great Vizier!

HERALD
Let all mouths close but mine.

[Lifting his staff.

The Holy, the Just, the High-born, the Omnipotent; the Gardener of the Vale of Islam, the Lion of the Imperial Forests, the Rider on the Spotless Horse, the Cyprus on the Golden Hill, the Master of Spears, the Redresser of Wrong, the Drinker of Blood, the Peacock of the World, the Shadow of God on Earth, the Commander of the Faithful, Haroun ar Raschid ben Mohammed, Ibn Abdullah Ibn Mohammed Ibn Ali ben Abdullah, Ibn 'Abbas, the Caliph.

SOLDIERS
The Holy, the High-born, the Just One, the Caliph!
The Cypress, the Peacock, the Lion, the Caliph!
From Rum to Bokhara one monarch, the Caliph!

DERVISH [Gloomily]
A clay thing, a plaything, a shadow, the Caliph!

CALIPH
The Divan is open. Let all mouths close but mine. Our justice today will be swift as a blow of the sword. In the Book of the Wisdom of Rulers I read: "Be sudden to uproot the tree of conspiracy for it scatters far its seed." Are you the Beggars?

BEGGARS
We are the beggars of Bagdad.

CALIPH
Thou, spokesman, come hither! Wherefore didst thou plot against my throne and the safety of all Islam? Didst thou not fear not only for thy life but for thy salvation?

BEGGAR
Master and Lord of the World, hast thou been poor, hast thou been hungry? Dost thou know what dreams enter the gaunt heads of starving men as they lie against the back of thy garden wall, and moan: "Bread in God's name, bread in the name of God?"

CALIPH
Dost thou deny conspiracy?

BEGGAR
I conspired.

CALIPH
Is there one of you denieth conspiracy?

[Silence.

Masrur, lead out the conspirators to death.

[**MASRUR** executes the order.

CALIPH
Let those whose duty it is fetch him who is called the King of the Beggars from his cell, and let him who did us the great service of capturing alive that dangerous man, step forth into the midst.

CHIEF OF POLICE [Stepping forward]
Lord of the World—but I am dirt.

CAPTAIN OF MILITARY [Simultaneously advancing]
Lord of the World—but I am dung.

CALIPH
Where you both concerned in his capture? My favour is doubled upon you.
Let two robes of honour be brought before my throne.

CHIEF OF POLICE
Sir, I fail to comprehend the presence of this military man.
He was but a spectator when I dragged out the King of Beggars from the gutter of his roof.

CAPTAIN OF MILITARY
O thou civilian, I caught a valiant hold of his legs, despite his heavy and continuous kicks, whilst thou didst but timidly pluck at his sleeve.

CHIEF OF POLICE

Pluck at his sleeve, tin-coated murderer! Summon the twenty drops of blood that trickle round thy lank and withered frame and let them mount to thy mendacious cheek!

CAPTAIN OF MILITARY
Thou dropsical elephant!

CALIPH
Enough! I love to hear the speech of heroes, but enough. It is clear the glory is divided. Give me one of those robes of honour, and summon the tailor of the court.

COURT TAILOR [Very prostrate]
O Master of the World, O Master!

CALIPH
Slit me this robe in twain.

COURT TAILOR [Moaning as he does so]
Allah is great, Allah is great.
Such a well-cut robe: such excellent silk!

CALIPH
Come hither both.

CAPTAIN OF MILITARY [Hanging back]
The glory is all to the police.

CHIEF OF POLICE
The credit is entirely due to my honourable friend.

CALIPH [Insisting]
Come hither both.

[They are fitted with half a robe of honour each amid laughter.

SOLDIERS
Long live those whom the Caliph delights to honour!

CAPTAIN OF MILITARY [Under his teeth]
Mutinous swine!

CALIPH
And now bring forth the King of the Beggars.

[The **KING OF THE BEGGARS** is brought in chained hand and foot, but still dressed in gold.

The Salaam to my host of yesternight.

RAFI, KING OF BEGGARS

The Salaam, O man of Basra. I see thy fellow-merchant in the robes of the Grand Vizier. But the negro, that most disgusting Negro, seems to be absent. To Hassan, my congratulations on his advancement.

CALIPH
Thou dost speak with the impudence of a king, but thy subjects are taken from thee. They will soon be black crows in the pine-wood by the walls.

RAFI
Had I but known thee last night, thou man of Basra, whom men call Caliph of the Faithful—O thou massacrer of good men—had I but known thee, had I but known thee!

CHIEF OF POLICE
Shall I tear out his tongue?

CALIPH
Let him talk. I have found a man who does not flatter me. Let me study
the hatred in his eyes.

RAFI
It is not enough for thee to misrule a quarter of the world.
Thou art not only a fool tyrant, but a mean tradesman, thou dog-hearted spy!

JAFAR
It is not decent to let this man continue his coarse abuse, O Master.
Wilt thou not end him?

CALIPH
He shall end in his time.
[To **KING OF THE BEGGARS**]
Thy impudence will not redound to thy advantage,
Rafi! Wherefore dost thou not bite the tongue of insolence
with the tooth of discretion?

RAFI
I am a man in the presence of death.

CALIPH
There a thousand paths to the delectable tavern of death, and some run straight and some run crooked.

RAFI
Cut, scourge, burn, rack thy uttermost. The nobler the aim the baser the failure. Do not I deserve to feel every separate pain of those whom my folly has sent to cruel death?

CHINESE PHILOSOPHER
I am a hundred and ten years old, and I have never heard a remark in more exquisite taste.

CALIPH

It is well. But before I send thee to a death so cruel that thy conscience will be fully satisfied in this world and the next, answer me this: Hast thou forgotten that unparalleled lady whom the zeal of my servants ravished from thy embrace?

RAFI
Thou devil of Eblis! Have I forgotten? Have I not prayed thou shouldst forget?

CALIPH
Shall a gallant man forget the name of a beautiful woman? We will look on her, for whom thou didst attempt to raze the central fort of Islam.
[To **ATTENDANTS**] Bring in this lady, Pervaneh.

RAFI [In supplication]
O Master of the World! O Master of the World!

CALIPH
Thou changest tone abruptly but late.

RAFI
I was insolent only that her name should be forgotten in thy anger and my death, O Splendour of Islam!

CALIPH
A crafty excuse for impoliteness. Wilt thou now begin to be polite to the tyrant whose coffin was to be nailed over his open eyes? He who hopes for his audience to forget the subject of his discourse should moderate his style.

RAFI
God blind me that I may not see her!

CALIPH
Why? Dost thou not love her still? Is not the sight of his beloved to the victim of separation like the vision of a fountain to him who dies of thirst?

HASSAN [Aside]
But if that fountain be a fountain whose drops are blood?

RAFI
Thou, thou hast held her in thy arms! O God, have pity on my soul!

CALIPH
But with this knowledge thou didst still desire her, and was ready
to wreck Bagdad for the sparkle of her eyes.

RAFI
But first the blood of her possessor should have washed her honour clean.

CALIPH

Thou art a most ridiculous man. Thou hast built thy monstrous tower of crime on a foundation of painted smoke. Dost thou imagine I have tasted all the fruit of my garden?

RAFI
Allah has given thee men's bodies, but it is for him alone to torment the soul. By thy faith, O Caliph, speak the truth!

CALIPH
Do I know every slave whom my industrious officials sweep in from the streets? To my knowledge I have never set my eyes on this woman of thine.

HERALD
The maiden Pervaneh!

CALIPH
Let her come before me.

[**PERVANEH** is ushered into the Presence.

PERVANEH [With due reverence]
O Master of the World!

CALIPH
It is written in the Sacred Law: In the King's presence a woman may unveil, without fear of censure.

PERVANEH
Ah, Master, but only the eagle dare look upon the sun.

CALIPH
Thy speech is proud enough for all the eagles, Lady Pervaneh, and I doubt not thy eyes, which I desire to see, are steady in the blaze of danger. Must I command thee to unveil?

PERVANEH
Alas, Master of the World, my eyes are dim with long confinement in a jewelled cage, and the wings of my soul are numb. Only on the hills of my country where the rolling sun of Heaven has his morning home, only on their windy hills do the women of my country go unveiled.

ISHAK [To himself, half singing]
The hills, the hills, the morning on the hills!

CALIPH [To **PERVANEH**]
I command thee to unveil.

PERVANEH
If thou wilt tear my veil off my face, I will tear my face before thy eyes.

RAFI
Ah, no!...

PERVANEH
Who art thou who dost cry, "Ah, no!"? Who art thou who dost hide thy face in fettered hands ...

RAFI
A prisoner.

PERVANEH
—dissembling thy voice...

RAFI
A prisoner awaiting death.

PERVANEH
—trembling when I touch thee?

RAFI
A man afraid.

PERVANEH [In a voice of exaltation]
For thee, Sultan, I raise my veil; and wait, thy captive, to share thy destiny.

HASSAN
Oh, Ishak! The fire of the heart of beauty!

RAFI
Leave me, Pervaneh! Walk not upon my path! You do not know what a foul doom is mine.

PERVANEH
Foul dooms? Foul dooms? Rafi, I can forget ten centuries of doom now that I see your eyes again!

RAFI
I conspired against his throne to win you freedom. Through my fault I failed, through my fault my thousand followers are dancing in the wind.

PERVANEH
For me you conspired? For me—for me?

RAFI
I would have drowned Bagdad in blood to kiss your lips again.

PERVANEH
O lover!

RAFI [Showing his fettered hands]
Lover indeed!

PERVANEH

There are a thousand eyes around us, O my beloved, but what care I? The voice of the world cries out, "Thou art a slave in the Palace, and thy lover a prisoner in chains."

[Embracing him.

But we have heard the Trumpets of Reality that drown the vain din of the Thing that Seems. We have walked with the Friend of Friends in the Garden of the Stars, and He is pitiable to poor lovers who are pierced by the arrows of this ghostly world. Your lips are the only lips, my lover, your eyes the only eyes—all the other eyes but phantom lights that glitter in the mist of dream.

COURTIER
This is sheer heresy.

ISHAK
Then a plague on your religion.

JAFAR
This is Sufic doctrine, and most dangerous to the State.

HASSAN
Then a plague on the State!

CALIPH
Ye who make love in full Divan, can ye yet listen to the voice of the world?

PERVANEH [Dazed]
They are speaking.

CALIPH
O Rafi, King of the Beggars, since after all thou art much entangled in the web of unreality, it is necessary that I ask thee some phantom questions concerning thy apparent acts.

Firstly, dost thou deny thou didst call thyself Caliph of the Unbelievers, and blaspheme thy faith in my presence and in the presence of Jafar, my Vizier, Masrur, the Executioner, and Hassan, my friend?

RAFI
I have nothing to deny.

CALIPH
Dost thou, secondly, deny that thou didst swear in the presence of the same to nail the Caliph of the Faithful alive in his coffin, or that thou didst conspire with the beggars to slay me, to seize Bagdad and to usurp the throne?

RAFI
I have nothing to deny.

CALIPH
Dost thou, thirdly, deny that thou didst scheme this monstrous crime for the sake of a woman?

RAFI
I have nothing to deny.

CALIPH
Rafi, thou art confessed a Blasphemer, a Traitor...and a Lunatic.
It remains to consider thy punishment.

RAFI
As thou wilt.

CALIPH
Thou art brave, but I fear the shafts of unreality will prick thee extremely hard. For thou hast merited not one but a dozen deaths. Now, if I impale thee for conspiracy, how shall I burn thee for blasphemy? But with such other pains as man can suffer, judicious arrangement carries the day over unthinking brutality. For if I skin thee for thy impudence, how can I flog thee for thy folly? But if the order is reversed thou canst enjoy the benefits of both expiations.

RAFI
Thou hast certainly studied the art of pain.

CALIPH
Yet what are the worst tortures thou shalt undergo to the horror of the death thou didst contrive for me?

RAFI [With impatience]
What is my condemnation?

CALIPH
For Lunacy to be nailed, for Conspiracy to be stretched, for Blasphemy to be split.

PERVANEH
Ah!

[Murmurs of horror and satisfaction fill the Court at the announcement of this savage punishment.

RAFI
As Allah wills.

PERVANEH [Falling at the **CALIPH**'s feet]
Spare, Spare, O Master of the World!

CALIPH
Dost thou think I will absolve him for thy "spare"?

PERVANEH
Mercy! Oh, Mercy!

CALIPH
Why dost thou cry "Mercy" and clasp my feet? Is not pain a fancy and this world a cloud?

PERVANEH [Rising to her feet]
This world is Hell, but those that dig Hell deeper shall find the Hell-beneath-the-Hells which they search for.

CALIPH
Thou hast metaphysic, but hast thou logic? Invent me a reason—one small and subtle reason—why I should show mercy to this man.

PERVANEH
Ah—wilt thou have reasons?

CALIPH
Was not my sentence just?

PERVANEH
Wilt thou have justice?

CALIPH
If I had stood bound before him, would he have listened to my prayer?

PERVANEH
Wilt thou have revenge?

CALIPH
Shall I scorn reason, pervert justice, and put aside revenge—for thy dark eyes?

PERVANEH
Turn thy justice, turn thy revenge on me in the name of the dark eyes of God! They say a woman suffers longer and sharper than a man.

CALIPH
Lady, dost thou mean this with all its meaning, or say it to implore pity?
Beware of thy answer! The rack and the whip are ready and near at hand.

PERVANEH [Her arms outstretched]
Then give the word. Knock off those fetters before my eyes—and nail me to the wall.

RAFI
Pervaneh!

CALIPH
Ecstasy! Ecstasy! Thou art an ecstatic and wilt not suffer.
I know the thick skin of martyrs. I refuse.

PERVANEH [To **RAFI**]

Alas, what can I do!

RAFI
Let me die! I have seen you again. It is nothing for a man to die.

PERVANEH
Nothing for a man to die? 'Tis Heaven wide open for a man to die.
But they will tear you, Rafi, Rafi!

RAFI
Shall I fear the pain you called upon yourself, or shrink where you were brave?

PERVANEH [To the **CALIPH**]
I ask so small a boon. Grant my lover a clean death!

CALIPH
Thou dost ask a very great boon indeed. For as thou sayest, what is death? Shall the man who shakes my kingdom slip into eternity like a thief men catch in the bazaar? Shall he who does the greater wrong not suffer the greater pain?

PERVANEH
He is not afraid of pain.

CALIPH
That is not to say he feels not pain.

PERVANEH
Just and reasonable, yet there is a holier thing than reason and justice.

DERVISH [His orthodoxy disturbed]
A holier thing than justice?

PERVANEH
Yes, Dervish. There is that which should not be defiled.

CALIPH
Whither now does thy plea wander?

PERVANEH
O Father of Islam, can thine eyes that love flowers behold man's body hewn into foul shapes and monstrous as the phantoms that go wailing round the graves? Can thy ears that love the music of Ishak, listen to the gasps of the tormented droning through their bodies like a winter wind among the pines?

CALIPH
I shall not honour Rafi with my attendance: I shall be far from sight and sound.

PERVANEH
The thought of it—the thought of it!

CALIPH
I have been ordering executions all my life. There is only one thought that can haunt me—the thought of a coffin closing on open eyes, the sway of the coffin carried to the grave, the crash at the bottom of the pit, the rumble of earth on the lid, the gasping for breath and light.

PERVANEH
He was distraught by passion, he spoke in fury: but thou dost judge him with a quiet mind. He is a man among men, but thou art the representative of God on earth, the sole Priest of Islam. Thou shalt not order God's image to be defiled.

CALIPH
So you would have me spare him for the sake of the perfection of man's body? O Pervaneh, I am far more likely to spare him for the perfection of woman's.

PERVANEH [Shrinking from the implied menace]
For those that have wits,
O Master, perfection is sundered from desire.

CALIPH
You are a woman—perfect—but a woman.

PERVANEH
By the curse of God.

CALIPH
And however much you sunder perfection from desire, from desire your perfection is not sundered.

PERVANEH
I am the slave of thy household to come or go, to fetch or to carry, to be struck or slain; but my perfection is not the slave of your desire.

CALIPH [Softly]
Yet if you return to my household...

PERVANEH [In fury]
To die.

CALIPH
You would not be forgotten or neglected...and your presence would be a consolation and a charm....

PERVANEH
Not to you, frigid tyrant, not to you!

CALIPH [Softly]
Nor yet to the one who let your lover go in peace?

PERVANEH

Is there no shame in the world of Islam? Will you unclothe your lust in full Divan?

CALIPH
You have already given the example. Come, shall I set your lover free?

PERVANEH
I would choke if you touched me, I would choke. Oh, the shame on me, the shame! You are smiling. It is not me you want but my shame! Is there a God in heaven that lets you sit and smile! But you can set him free. Ah, will you set him free? I am your slave—I am your slave. You can rob me of rope and knife—the very means of death. If you will set him free! I am your slave, what choice have I?

CALIPH
Thou hast not the manners or the heart of a slave. Thou wast brought to my household by violence, a free woman born, and art no slave of mine. In the presence of my Divan I pronounce thee free. Thou art free to come and free to go, free to buy and free to sell, free to walk out or free to stay, free to wed and free to die—and free to make a choice....

PERVANEH
To make a choice? What choice? Between his death and my dishonour?

CALIPH
No, between love and life.

PERVANEH
Explain, O Master of the World.

CALIPH
Between two deaths with torment and two lives with a separation.
Between a day of love and all the years of life.

PERVANEH
Enlighten my understanding.

CALIPH
I have considered this matter. I have decided this matter.
I will speak plain and clear.
[Rising]
This is my irrevocable judgment from which there is no appeal. I give a choice to Pervaneh and Rafi, the King of the Beggars, and I grant them till sunset to consult their hearts and make that choice together. They shall both live on these conditions: that the lady Pervaneh return forthwith to my harem to be my wife in lawful wedlock, and be treated with all the honour her boldness and her beauty merit. That the King of the Beggars leave Bagdad, and that these two lovers part for ever till they die.

But if they refuse this separation, I offer them one day of love, from sunset to-night to sunset on the morrow, unfettered and alone, with no more guard than may keep them from self-destruction. But when that day is over they shall die together in merciless torment.

In the name of Allah the most merciful, the Divan is closed.

ACT IV

SCENE I

In the vaults of the palace, outside the cell of the **KING OF THE BEGGARS**.

[Enter **HASSAN**.

HASSAN
Which way? Which way? I am lost in this dark passage. My voice rings around the arches. What's that noise? Is there an army coming? Or are all the prisoners stamping with wrath?...No....It is only someone walking....I wonder who! And if this stranger asks me my business what shall I say to him? Do I know what brought me to this dismal region?

ISHAK [From the darkness]
Who goes there? Who goes there? What dost thou here?
What is thy business?

HASSAN
Who calls? I am Hassan, inspecting the security of the imperial prisons.
Who art thou?

ISHAK
Who am I? Ten books were written by Aflatun and twenty by Aristu to answer that mighty question, O Hassan of my heart.

HASSAN
Ishak! Come out of hiding, Ishak. What are you doing here?

ISHAK
I gather mushrooms, O inspector of the vaults of vice!

HASSAN Have you come too? I do not know why I came. I hoped...I do not know why I came, but I think our hearts do beat together like the hearts of friends. Did you come here because of them?

ISHAK
I came here to hear a play more tragic than the mysteries of Hossein, to listen to a debate more weighty than the council talk of kings....

HASSAN
You do not mean?...

ISHAK
I mean the debate of love and life.

HASSAN
Could you spy on that? How cruel!

ISHAK
The poet must learn what man's agony can teach him.

HASSAN
Is it then not better not to be a poet?

ISHAK [Bitterly]
Allah did not ask me that question when he made me a poet and a dissector of souls. It is my trade: I do but follow my master, the exalted Designer of human carpets, the Ruler of the world. If he prepared the situation, shall I not observe the characters? Thus I corrupt my soul to create—Allah knoweth what—ten little words like rubies in a row. As for you, I think you begin to understand the Caliph of the Faithful.

HASSAN
Why speak of him? All men are brutes, you and he and I.
I thought that I was kinder than other men—but I was only more afraid.
This day is the first day of my exaltation, I have begun it the all but murderer of a woman, and I end it a spy on souls in trouble.

ISHAK
Do not worry any longer, dear Hassan, on the moral problem.
The moths of curiosity will always flutter round the lamp of circumstances.
Here comes the Guard, they shall direct us.

[Enter **TWO GUARDS**.

ISHAK [To the **GUARD**]
Ho, soldier, whither?

1st GUARD [Saluting]
To the cell of the King of the Beggars, my masters, to relieve the Guard.

ISHAK
What, will you stand inside the cell?

1st GUARD
Inside, O my masters.

ISHAK
A shame, I say, a shame to spy on a pair of lovers. Will they fly off through the keyhole?

1st GUARD
We know the ways of prisoners, O my masters. Masrur is disappointed when we bring him corpses to be whipped.
[To **2nd GUARD**]
Is he not disappointed, Mohamed?

2nd GUARD [In deep, lugubrious and respectful tones]
Oh, sir, he is bitterly disappointed.

ISHAK
Well, it is your fault, my fine fellows, if you leave daggers and ropes lying about in your prisoners' cells.

1st GUARD
Ah, you do not know the artfulness of prisoners, my masters.
They will bang their heads against the wall, or they will eat their straw.
[To **2nd GUARD**]
Do they not eat their straw, Mohamed?

2nd GUARD [To **ISHAK**]
Oh sir, they frequently eat their straw.

ISHAK
Chain them, chain them.

1st GUARD
We do, my masters, but even then they strangle themselves in their fetters.

ISHAK
Strangle themselves in their fetters?

1st GUARD
Do they not strangle themselves in their fetters, Mohamed.

2nd GUARD [To **ISHAK**]
I have known them, sir, to strangle themselves in their fetters.

ISHAK
But, as you know, these two have a choice between a life with separation and a death with torment. Now surely they will choose life, and will hardly need a sentry to spear them away from the doorstep of eternity.

1st GUARD
I should think so indeed, sir. But you never can tell with prisoners.
Prisoners are very obstinate, especially women, are they not Mohamed?

2nd GUARD [To **ISHAK**]
Female prisoners are very obstinate, sir.

ISHAK [With assumed heartiness]
Well, none of us would require till sunset to make our choice, would we?

1st GUARD
No, sir, not those of us who have ever seen Masrur at work.

ISHAK
But if they do choose their day of love, will they still not be free according to the Caliph's promise? Will you still guard them in their cell, O sons of impropriety, lest they eat their straw?

1st GUARD [With a leer]
Nay, we shall stand outside the door and listen at the grill.

ISHAK
And that is precisely what we intend to do now if you will show us the door.

1st GUARD
I don't know whether I could quite do that, sir.

ISHAK [Giving him money]
You are valiant fellows and, I am convinced, considerably underpaid.

1st GUARD
Ours is a most disagreeable profession. your Excellency.

2nd GUARD [Accepting money]
And the emoluments are infinitesimal.

1st GUARD
This way, gentlemen.

[Shews them to the door.

SCENE II

A cell. A grating through which streams the sunlight. A heavy door with a narrow spyhole. **RAFI** is fettered to the wall, but **PERVANEH** has not been bound. **TWO GUARDS** stand immobile on either side of the door,

RAFI
They have changed our guard for the last time, it will be sunset in an hour.

PERVANEH
Still a long hour before your hands are freed to make me a belt of love.
O idle sun, I am weary of thy pattern on the wall. Still a long hour!

RAFI
And still a night and a day before our doom.

PERVANEH

Why is your voice so sorrowful? Your words do not keep step with your decision nor march like standard-bearers of your great resolve.

PERVANEH
What have I decided? What have I resolved? You came near. I saw the wings of your spirit beating the air around you. You locked the silver fetters around my neck and I forgot these manacles of iron: you perfumed me with your hair till this cell became a meadow: you turned toward me eyes in whose night the seven deep oceans flashed their drowned stars, and all your body asked without speech, "Wilt thou die for love?"

PERVANEH
Do you repent? Do you unsay the golden words?

RAFI
Put but your lips on mine and seal my words against unsaying.

PERVANEH
I did wrong to make you passionate. I see that in your heart you do repent. I would not have you bound by a moment's madness but wish with all your reason and with all your soul.

RAFI
Ah, stand apart and veil your face, you who call in the name of reason! You are all afire for martyrdom: can you hear reason calling from her snows? Oh, you woman, Allah curse you for blinding my eyes with love!

PERVANEH
Ah, Rafi!

RAFI
Be silent—be silent! Your voice is the voice of a garden at daybreak, when all the birds are singing at the sun. Forget your whirling dreams, your fires, your lightnings, your splendours of the soul, and answer the passionless voice that asks you—why should your lover die, and such a death?

PERVANEH
I am listening.

RAFI
I am very young. Shall I forget to laugh if I continue to live? Shall I spend all my hours regretting you? Shall I not return to my country and comfort the hearts of those that gave me birth? Have I not my white-walled house, my books, my old friends, my garden of flowers and trees? Has the stream forgotten to sing at the end of my garden because Pervaneh comes no more?

"Love fades," saith Reason, with a gentler voice. "Love fades but doth not fall. Love fadeth not to yellow like the rose but to gold like the leaves upon the poplar by the stream." And when my poplars are all gold, I shall sit beneath their shade beside the stream to read my book. When I am tired of my book I will lie on my back and watch the clouds. There in the clouds I shall see your face, and remember you with a wistful remembrance as if you had always been a dream and the silver torment of your arms had never been more than the white mists circling the round mountain snows.

PERVANEH [With growing anger]
And so, wrapped in pleasant fancies, you will forget the woman you have sold to a tyrant. And so, while I, far from my country and my home, am dying of shame and confinement, you will dream and you will dream!

RAFI
The plague on your dishonour! You are to be the Caliph's wife.
Is that not held for the highest honour to which a woman can attain?
Is that worse shame than being flayed by a foul negro? The shame! the selling! the dishonour! A woman's vanity: am I to be tortured to death to gratify your pride? If I must not have you, do I care whose wife you are? I shall remember you as you are now—rock water undefiled.

PERVANEH
Cold and heartless coward; you are afraid of death!

RAFI
By Allah, I am afraid of death, and the man who fears not death is a dullard and a fool! Are we still making speeches in full Divan to the admiration of the by-standers? Must we pose even now! If you hate me for fearing death, go your way and leave this coward. Ah, no, no, do not leave me, O Pervaneh! Forgive me that I am what I am. I have not unsaid my promise. I will die with you. I will die! I will endure the tortures that are thrice as terrible as death, the tortures that parch my mouth with fear.

PERVANEH
Shame on you, weak and shivering lover! What is pain for us?

RAFI
You do not see—you do not see! Look at your hands, they shall be torn—ah, I cannot speak of it. I shall see your blood flow like wine from a white fountain drop by drop till you have painted the carpet of execution all red lilies.

PERVANEH
Ah—but will not even your poor love flow deep when I set that crimson seal upon the story of our lives!

RAFI
Alas, you are still dreaming: you are still blind with exaltation: your speech is a metaphor. You do not see, you have never heard the high, thin shriek of the tortured, you have not seen the shape of their bodies when they are cast into the ditch. Come near, Pervaneh. Do you know what they will do to you? Come near: I cannot say it aloud.

[**PERVANEH** approaches.

Ah, I dare not tell you...I dare not tell you!

PERVANEH
Tell me, plain and clear.

[**RAFI** whispers in **PERVANEH**'s ear...

PERVANEH [Covering her face with her hands]
Ah, God—they will not do that!
No, no; they will not do that to me.

RAFI
Pitilessly.

PERVANEH [Wildly]
They will do that!—Ah, the shame of it! They will do that—
Ah the pain of it! I see! I feel! I hear! O save me, Rafi!

RAFI
Alas! Why did I tell you this?

PERVANEH
It is beyond endurance: it is foul: my veins will burst at the very thought. I am between a shame and a shame and there is no escape....But at least they shall not do this to you, Rafi. Hush...talk low: the soldiers must not hear.

[Glancing at the **GUARDs** and whispering low.

Will you die here between my hands, instantly, and with no pain?

RAFI [In a hushed voice]
Quickly! How can you do it? We are guarded—have you a knife?

PERVANEH
My hands will be cunning round your neck, beloved. Did I not say you should die between my hands?

RAFI
Be quick: be quiet: I will cast back my head.

A GUARD [Thrusting **PERVANEH** back with his drawn sword as she lays her hands on her lover's neck]
Back, in the Caliph's name!

RAFI [To **PERVANEH**]
Run in upon his sword....

PERVANEH [Shrinking away from the **GUARD's** sword]
I cannot!

RAFI
Quick—quick! Fall on the sword and save all shame.

PERVANEH
My breast, my breast: I am afraid...

[Prostrate on the ground.

I am utterly shamed—I have missed your death and mine.

RAFI
You have flinched.

PERVANEH
The point was on my breast, and it might have been all ended for you and me.

RAFI
You have been afraid.

PERVANEH
It would have driven to my heart. Ah, the woman that I am!

RAFI
It is so small a thing, a pricking of the steel.

PERVANEH
Ah!—it is a little thing, you say? It is like ice, so sharp and cold.
I am a vile coward.

RAFI
We are both cowards, you and I. The sunlight changes on the wall from white to gold. It is evening. Our time has come. Shall we choose life? Shall we choose the sky and the sea, the mountains, the rivers and the plains? Shall we choose the flowers and the bees, and all the birds of heaven? Shall we choose laughter and tears, sorrow and desire, speech and silence, and the shout of the man behind the hill?

PERVANEH
Ah, empty, empty without your heart!

[She weeps.

RAFI
Empty as death, Pervaneh, empty as death?

PERVANEH
The wall reddens: the last minute has come: we must choose.

RAFI
Choose for me: I follow. Did I talk of life? My heart is breaking for desire of you. If you bid me depart I will not live without you. Choose for me—and choose well. Phantoms of pain! Let me but have you in my arms, and one day of love shall widen into eternity. Who knows? The earth may crack to-night, or the sun stay down for ever in his grave. Who knows—tomorrow—God will begin and finish the judgment of the world—and when it is all over find you sleeping in my arms?

PERVANEH [Rising slowly to her feet and laying her hands on the shoulders of her lover]

Oh, let us die! Not for my dishonour, Rafi.
What is my dishonour to me or to you, beloved, or the shame of a girl's virginity to him who made the sea? This clay of mine is fair enough, I think, but God hath cast it in the common mould. O lover, lover, I would walk beneath the walls and sell my body to the gipsy and the Jew ere you should cry "I am hungry" or "I am cold."

RAFI
Die for love of me—for a day and a night of love!

PERVANEH
I die for love of you, Rafi! Behold, the Spirit grows bright around you: you are one with the Eternal Lover, the Friend of the World. His spirit flashes in thine eyes and hovers round thy lips: thy body is all fire!

RAFI
Comfort me, comfort me! I do not understand thy dreams.

PERVANEH [Her arms stiffening in ecstasy]
The splendour pours from the window—the spirits in red and gold. Death with thee, O lover, death for thee, death to attain thee, O lover—and then the garden—then the fountain—then the walking side by side.

RAFI
O my sweet life, O my sweet life—must this mad dreaming end thee?

PERVANEH
Sweet life—we die for thy sweetness, O Lord of the Garden of Peace. Come, love, and die for the fire that beats within us, for the air that blows around us, for the mountains of our country and the wind among their pines you and I accept torture and confront our end. We are in the service of the World. The voice of the rolling deep is shouting: "Suffer that my waves may moan." The company of the stars sing out: "Be brave that we may shine." The spirits of children not yet born whisper as they crowd around us: "Endure that we may conquer."

RAFI
Pervaneh, Pervaneh!

PERVANEH
Hark! Hark!—down through the spheres—the Trumpeter of Immortality! "Die, lest I be shamed, lovers. Die, lest I be shamed!"

RAFI
Die then, Pervaneh, for thy great reasons. Me no ecstasy can help through the hours of pain. I die for love alone.

HERALD [Entering]
The Caliph demands your choice.

RAFI

Death!

HASSAN [Bursting in]
No, no. O God!

ISHAK
They have chosen too well.

[Exit **HERALD**. **PERVANEH** is still in ecstasy when the curtain falls.

ACT V

SCENE I

Towards the sunset of the next day. The **CALIPH**'s garden (ACT III, SCENE I) once more.

[Enter the **CALIPH** with **ATTENDANTS** as **HASSAN** comes from his pavilion.

CALIPH
We were coming to your door to seek you, Hassan, but you anticipated the knock of doubt by the shock of appearance. Why have you left your house before the nightingale? Will you too sing to the dawning moon? If so—we have come to hear.

HASSAN
Oh, Master of the World—the hour of the nightingale has not yet come. I have sought thee all day, O Master, and could not find thee. Thou didst hold the Divan—thou wast hunting—thou wast asleep—thou wast at dinner—and now the hour is near, O Master of the World—but not yet come.

CALIPH
What hour?

HASSAN
The hour of the nightingale: the hour when sun and moon are weighed in the silver scales of heaven: and thy scale of justice moves downward with the sun.

CALIPH
Surely thy head is full of fancies and thy mood perverse. I cannot grasp the shadow of thy meaning.

HASSAN [Throwing himself at the **CALIPH**'s feet]
O Master of the World, have mercy on Pervaneh and Rafi!

CALIPH
What—those two? Let them have mercy on themselves. They have chosen death as I am told. The woman has paid me the compliment of preferring torture with her Rafi to a marriage with myself. They have had a pleasant day together. Exquisite food was placed before them and the surveillance was discreet. They will now pass a less pleasant evening.

HASSAN
Let not the woman be tortured: have mercy on the woman.

CALIPH
Rise you fantastic supplicant. Do you dare ask mercy for these insolent and dangerous folk whose life was in their own hands—who have themselves pulled down the cord of the rat-trap of destruction?

HASSAN
Had you but heard them—had you but watched as I did while they made that awful choice, you would have forgotten expediency, justice, revenge, and listened only to the appeal of the anguish of their souls!

CALIPH
I doubt it!

HASSAN
They chose so well! They are so young. So terribly in love. I have not slept, I have not eaten, Master! I take no pleasure in my house and garden. I see blood on my walls, blood on my carpet, blood in the fountain, blood in the sky!

CALIPH
Well, well, I will leave you to these agreeable delusions. Abu Nawas has found me a young Kurdish girl who can dance with one leg round her neck, and knows by heart the song of Alexander. I perceive you will be no fit companion for an evening's sport.

HASSAN
It is only for the torture I speak: it is only for the woman I implore.
Say but one word: the sun will set so soon.

CALIPH [Angrily]
If thou and Ishak, and Jafar and the Governors of all the provinces were prostrate with supplication before me, I would not spare her one caress of Masrur's black hand.

HASSAN [Springing to his feet and making at the **CALIPH**]
Hideous tyrant, torturer from Hell!

CALIPH [Coolly, as **GUARDS** seize **HASSAN**]
You surprise me. Since when have confectioners become so tigerish in their deportment?

HASSAN [Terrified]
What have I said! What have I done!

CALIPH
There speaks the old confectioner again.

HASSAN
I am not ashamed to be a confectioner, but I am ashamed to be a coward.

CALIPH

Do not despair, good Hassan. You would not take my warning: you have left the Garden of Art for the Palace of Action: you have troubled your head with the tyranny of princes, and the wind of complication is blowing through your shirt. You will forfeit your house and be banished from the Garden, for you are not fit to be the friend of kings. But for the rest, since you did me great service the other night, go in peace, and all the confectionery of the Palace will be ordered at your shop.

HASSAN

Master, for this mercy, I thank you humbly.

CALIPH

For nothing—for nothing. I make allowance for the purple thread of madness woven in the camel-cloth of your character. I know your head is affected by a caloric afternoon. Indeed, I sympathise with the interest you have shown as to the fate of Pervaneh and Rafi, and as a mark of favour I offer you a place among the spectators of their execution.

HASSAN

Ah, no, no!—that I could never bear to see!

CALIPH

Moreover, as a special token of my esteem, I will not send you to the execution—I will bring the execution here, and have it held in your honour. You dreamt that your walls were sweating blood. I will fulfil the prophecy implied and make the dream come true.

HASSAN

I shall never sleep again!

CALIPH [To **ATTENDANT**]

Take my ring; go to the postern gate, intercept the procession of Protracted Death, and bid Masrur bring his prisoners to this pavilion and slay them on the carpet he shall find within the walls.

HASSAN

Master! Master! Is it not enough? I must go back to my trade and the filth of the Bazaar: I must be a poor man again and the fool of poor men. "Look at Hassan," men will say, "he has had his day of greatness: look at that greasy person: he has been clothed in gold: let us therefore go and insult the man who was once the Caliph's friend: let us draw moral lessons from him on the mutability of human affairs." But I, disregarding their jeers and insolent compassion, wrapping my body in my cloak and my soul in contemplation, would have remembered my day of pride, this Garden of Great Peace, this Fountain of Charm, this Pavilion of Beatitude: I would have recollected that I once had talked with Poets of the art of poetry, and owned slaves as pretty as their names. Preserve, preserve for me, O Master of the World, this palm-grove of memory in the desert of my affliction. Defile not this happy place with blood. Let not the trees that heard thee but yesterday call me Friend bow their heads beneath the wind of anguish: let not the threshold which I have crossed blossom out with blood! Spare me, spare me from hearing that which will haunt me for ever and ever—the moan of that white woman!

CALIPH [To **GUARDS**]

Do not release him till the end. See that he keeps his eyes well opened, and feasts them to the fill.

[Exit **CALIPH** and train.

[The song of the **MUEZZIN** is heard, "La Allah illa Allah," etc.

HASSAN
The sun has set. Guards, O Guards! [No answer] It is the hour of prayer, do you not pray? I have still a little treasure.

[No answer from the **GUARDS**.

Are you dumb?

[**GUARDS** nod.

But why are you not deaf?

[**GUARDS** point to their tongues.

Ah—your tongues have been torn out!

[**GUARD** points to window of the pavilion.

What do you point at?... Ah, Yasmin!

YASMIN
I have seen and heard behind the lattice. Hassan has fallen from power and favour.

HASSAN [Crazily]
Ah, good, very good, surpassing good!
You are at the window—I am in the street. This is a reflection of that.
As swans go double in a river, so do events come drifting down our lives. Again, again!
Bow down thy head, O burning bright! for one night or the other night
Will come the gardener in white, and gathered flowers are dead, Yasmin!

Come now, a sweet lie first, Yasmin: sing a little how you love me.
Show me your beauty limb by limb—then bring, ah, bring your new lover—mock my moon-touched verses and call me the fool, the old fool, the weary fool I am.

YASMIN
I will not yet call Hassan a fool. Hassan has fallen from power, but he need not fall from riches. The Palace Confectioner Hassan, may still become the richest merchant in Bagdad.

HASSAN
Thou harlot, thou harlot, thou harlot!

YASMIN
Why art thou angry? In what have I insulted thee?

HASSAN
Oh, if it were thou about to suffer! If it were thou!

YASMIN [Staring across the garden and forgetting **HASSAN**]
At last, at last!—the Procession of Protracted Death! I shall see it all!

[A deep red afterglow illumines the back of the garden. Across the garden towards the door of the pavilion moves in black silhouettes the Procession of Protracted Death, of which the order is this:
MASRUR, naked, with his scimitar.
FOUR ASSISTANT TORTURERS in black holding steel implements.
TWO MEN in armour bearing a lighted brazier slung between them on a pole.
TWO MEN bearing a monstrous wheel.
FOUR MEN carrying the rack.
A MAN with a hammer and a whip.
PERVANEH and **RAFI**, half naked, pulling a cart that bears their coffins: their legs drag great chains. Behind each of them walks a soldier with uplifted sword.

MASRUR knocks at the door of the Pavilion: the **SLAVES** open and flee in terror at the sight. The light of the brazier glows through the window. The **SOLDIERS** who guard **PERVANEH** and **RAFI** unhook the chains that chain them to the cart, and placing their hands on the necks of the prisoners push them in. The four **SLAVES** of the house then appear under the guidance of the man with the whip and lift in the coffins. Lastly, **HASSAN** is taken by his two **GUARDS** and forced to enter. The stage grows absolutely dark, save for the shining of the light from the windows. In the silence rises the splashing of the fountain and the whirring and whirling of a wheel. The sounds blend and grow unendurably insistent, and with them music begins to play softly. A cry of pain is half smothered by the violins. At last the silver light of the moon floods the garden.

HASSAN, thrust forth by his **GUARDS**, appears at the door of the pavilion. His face is white and haggard: he totters a few steps and finally falls in a faint in the shadow of the fountain. The coffins are brought out, nailed down, and placed in a cart.

The **SOLDIERS** pull the cart in place of the prisoners, and what remains of the procession departs in reverse order. **MASRUR** only has lingered by the door. **YASMIN** is clutching at his arm.

YASMIN
Masrur—thou dark Masrur.

MASRUR
Allah—the woman.

YASMIN
How you smell of blood.

MASRUR
And you of roses.

YASMIN

I laughed to see them writhe—I laughed, I laughed, as I watched behind the curtain. Why did you drink his veins?

MASRUR
A vow.

YASMIN
Will you not drink mine also?

MASRUR
Shall I put my arms around you?

YASMIN
Your arms are walls of black and shining stone.
Your breast is the castle of the night.

MASRUR
Little white moth, I will crush you to my heart.

YASMIN [With a sudden cry of terror, struggling from his embrace a moment after]
Ah, let me go. Do you hear them?... Do you hear them?...

MASRUR
What is there to hear but the noises of the night?

YASMIN [Springing away]
The flowers are talking...the garden is alive...

[She falls.

MASRUR [Stooping the carry her]
She loves blood and is frightened of the moon.
She is smooth and white, I will take her home.

[Enter **ISHAK** searching for **HASSAN**.

ISHAK
Hassan—where doth he lie? Hassan, O Hassan.
Thou hast broken that gentle heart, Haroun, and I have broken my lute:
I play no more for thee. Ah, why did they not tell me sooner—I fear his reason may have fled before I find him: he may be wandering in the streets to-night like Death, and tearing at his eyes. Hassan, oh, Hassan! It is he: he lies just as I first saw him: beneath a fountain, face toward the moon. His life is rhyming like a song: it harks back to the old refrain. Is life a mirror wherein events show double?

HASSAN [Half waking from his swoon]
Swans that drift into the mist....

ISHAK [Bending over him to raise him]

Friend, I am glad to hear thy voice.
Rise, rise, thou art in a pitiable case.

HASSAN [Faintly]
Let me lie....This place is quiet, and the earth smells cool.
May I never rise till they lift me aboard my coffin, and I'll go a sailing down the river and out to sea.

ISHAK
You are alive—no one will hurt you: you hold to your reason and fight despair.

HASSAN
And in that sea are no red fish....

ISHAK
Come: rise: be brave: I know you have suffered.

HASSAN
She was brave. Ah, her hands, her hands!

ISHAK
Do not tell me that tale.

HASSAN
You are a poet. They cut off her lover's head and poured blood upon her eyes!

ISHAK
Be silent. You are full of devils. I tell you, it is not true.
Stop dreaming: look into my eyes: listen!

[Bells are heard without the garden.

You hear? The camels are being driven to the Gate of the Moon. At midnight starts the great summer caravan for the cities of the Far North East, divine Bokhara and happy Samarkand. It is a desert path as yellow as the bright sea-shore: therefore the Pilgrims call it The Golden Journey.

HASSAN
And what of that to you or me, your Golden Journey to Samarkand?

ISHAK
I am leaving this city of slaves, this Bagdad of fornication. I have broken my lute and will write no more qasidahs in praise of the generosity of kings. I will try the barren road, and listen for the voice of the emptiness of earth. And you shall walk beside me.

HASSAN
I?

ISHAK
Rise, and confide to me once more the direction of your way.

HASSAN [Rising with **ISHAK**'s aid]
Why save me from a death desired?
What am I to you or to any man living?
Why would you force me like a fate to live?

ISHAK
Because I am your friend, and need you.

HASSAN
Oh, Ishak, singer of songs!

ISHAK
Prepare for travel.

HASSAN
I have no possessions.

ISHAK
O pilgrim! O true pilgrim! I have dinars of gold: we will furnish ourselves at the gate, and change these silks of indolence for the camel-hair of toil. But have you not one thing in your house to take—no one single thing?

HASSAN [With a great shudder]
Within that door—nothing.
But I have one old carpet that still lies in my shop.
Its gentle flowers the negro has not defiled.
And yet I dare not seek it.

ISHAK
I will bring it you. You shall stretch it out upon the desert when you say your evening prayer, and it will be a little meadow in the waste of sand.

HASSAN [Seizing **ISHAK** on a sudden panic]
Keep close to me: do not leave me!
The night is growing wild!

ISHAK
Hold to your reason! It is all stars and moon and crystal peace.

HASSAN
The trees are moving without a wind...the flowers are talking... the stars are growing bigger....

ISHAK
Be calm, there is nothing.

[The fountain runs red.

HASSAN
The fountain—the fountain!

ISHAK
Oh! alas! it is pouring blood! Come away.

HASSAN
The Garden is alive!

ISHAK
Come away: it is haunted! Come away: come away! Follow the bells!

[Exeunt in terror.

[The **GHOST** of the Artist of the Fountain rises from the fountain itself in pale Byzantine robes.

FOUNTAIN GHOST
The garden to the ghosts. Come forth, new brother and new sister. Come forth while enough of earth's heavy influence remains upon you—to speak and to be seen. Come forth, and those who are past shall dance with those who are to come.

GHOST OF RAFI [With the voice of **RAFI**, the clothes of **RAFI**, the broken fetters of **RAFI**, but pale...as death]
We are here, O Shadow of the Fountain.

FOUNTAIN GHOST
Welcome, thou and thy white lady to these...haunts.
Wander at will. I have scared away the sons of flesh.

GHOST OF RAFI
How were they scared, those two?

FOUNTAIN GHOST
When the water turned from white to red their faces turned from red to white. They ran!

GHOST HIDDEN IN THE TREES
Ha! ha!

GHOST OF PERVANEH
Tell us, O Man of the Fountain, what shall we do?

FOUNTAIN GHOST
Nothing: you are dead.

GHOST OF PERVANEH
Shall we stay in this garden and be lovers still, and fly in the air and flit among the leaves?

FOUNTAIN GHOST

As long as you remember what you suffered, you will stay near the house where your blood was shed.

GHOST OF PERVANEH
We will remember that ten thousand years.

FOUNTAIN GHOST
You have forgotten that you are a Spirit.
The memories of the dead are thinner than their dreams.

GHOST OF PERVANEH
But you stay here, by the fountain.

FOUNTAIN GHOST
I created the fountain: what have you created in the world?

GHOST OF PERVANEH
Nothing but the story of our lives.

FOUNTAIN GHOST
That will not save you. You were spiritual even in life.
I see it by the great shadows of your eyes.
But I cared only for the earth. I loved the veins of the leaves, the shapes of crawling beasts, the puddle in the road, the feel of wood and stone. I knew the shapes of things so well that my sculpture was the best in the world. Therefore my spirit is still heavy with memories of earth and I stay in the world I love. Do I desire to see the back of the moon?

GHOST OF PERVANEH
May not we stay also? May I not touch the shadow of his lips and hear the whisper of his love? Shall we be driven from here, O Man of the fountain?

FOUNTAIN GHOST
How do I know? Can I foresee?

GHOST OF PERVANEH
Thou, too dost not foresee. But what of Paradise, what of Infinity—what of the stars, and what of us?

FOUNTAIN GHOST
I know no more than you.

GHOST OF PERVANEH
Is the secret secret still, and this existence darker than the last?

FOUNTAIN GHOST
Didst thou hope for a revelation? Why should the dead be wiser than the living? The dead know only this—that it was better to be alive.

GHOST OF PERVANEH
But we shall feel no more pain—Oh, no more pain, Rafi!

FOUNTAIN GHOST
But you will feel so cold.

GHOST OF PERVANEH
With the fire of love within us?

FOUNTAIN GHOST
You will forget when the wind blows.

GHOST OF PERVANEH
Forget! Rafi, Rafi, shall we forget, Rafi?

GHOST OF RAFI [In a thin voice like an echo]
Forget...Rafi...

FOUNTAIN GHOST
You will forget, when the great wind blows you asunder and you are borne on it with ten million others like drops on a wave of air.

GHOST OF PERVANEH
There is a faith in me that tells I shall not forget my lover though God forget the world. And where will the wind take us?

FOUNTAIN GHOST
What do I know, or they? I only know it rushes.

GHOST OF PERVANEH
How do you know about the wind?

FOUNTAIN GHOST
Because it blows through the garden and drives the souls together.

GHOST OF PERVANEH
What souls?

FOUNTAIN GHOST
The souls of the unborn children who live in the flowers.

GHOST OF PERVANEH
And how do you know about the passage of ten million souls?

FOUNTAIN GHOST
They pass like a comet across the midnight skies.

GHOST OF PERVANEH
Phantoms shall not make me fear. But what of Justice and Punishment and Reason and Desire? What of the Lover in the Garden of Peace?

FOUNTAIN GHOST
Ask of the wind.

GHOST OF PERVANEH
I shall be answered: I know that in the end I shall find the Lover in the Garden of Peace.

VOICES
And what of Life?

GHOST OF PERVANEH
Who asks, What of Life?

FOUNTAIN GHOST
The spirits of those who will soon be born.

VOICES
We have left our flowers. We know we shall soon be born.
What of Life, O dead?

GHOST OF PERVANEH [With a great cry]
Why, Life...is sweet, my children!

[The leaves of the trees begin to rustle.

FOUNTAIN GHOST
Listen to the tress.

GHOST OF PERVANEH
Is it coming?

FOUNTAIN GHOST
It is the wind. I must go down into the earth.

[The **FOUNTAIN GHOST** vanishes.

GHOST OF PERVANEH
Ah, I am cold—I am cold—beloved!

GHOST OF RAFI [Scarce visible and very faint]
Cold...cold.

GHOST OF PERVANEH
Speak to me, speak to me, Rafi.

GHOST OF RAFI
Rafi—Rafi—who was Rafi?

GHOST OF PERVANEH
Speak to thy love—thy love—thy love.

GHOST OF RAFI
Cold...cold...cold.

[The wind sweeps the **GHOSTS** out of the garden, seeming also to ring more wildly the bells of the Caravan.

SCENE II

At the Gate of the Moon, Bagdad. Blazing moonlight. **MERCHANTS**, **CAMEL-DRIVERS** and their beasts, **PILGRIMS**, **JEWS**, **WOMEN**, all manner of people. By the barred gate stands the **WATCHMAN** with a great key. Among the pilgrims, **HASSAN** and **ISHAK** in the robes of pilgrims.

THE MERCHANTS [Together]
Away, for we are ready to a man!
Our camels sniff the evening and are glad.
Lead on, O Master of the Caravan,
Lead on the Merchant-Princes of Bagdad.

THE CHIEF DRAPER
Have me not Indian carpets dark as wine,
Turbans and sashes, gowns and bows and veils,
And broideries of intricate design,
And printed hangings in enormous bales?

THE CHIEF GROCER
We have rose-candy, we have spikenard,
Mastic and terebinth and oil and spice,
And such sweet jams meticulously jarred
As God's Own Prophet eats in Paradise.

THE PRINCIPAL JEWS:
And we have manuscripts in peacock styles
By Ali of Damascus: we have swords
Engraved with storks and apes and crocodiles,
And heavy beaten necklaces for lords.

THE MASTER OF THE CARAVAN
But you are nothing but a lot of Jews

PRINCIPAL JEW
Sir, even dogs have daylight, and we pay.

MASTER OF THE CARAVAN

But who are ye in rags and rotten shoes,
You dirty-bearded, blocking up the way?

ISHAK
We are the Pilgrims, master; we shall go
Always a little further; it may be
Beyond that last blue mountain barred with snow
Across that angry or that glimmering sea,

White on a throne or guarded in a cave
There lies a prophet who can understand
Why men were born: but surely we are brave,
Who take the Golden Road to Samarkand.

THE CHIEF MERCHANTS
We gnaw the nail of hurry. Master, away!

ONE OF THE WOMEN
O turn your eyes to where your children stand.
Is not Bagdad the beautiful? O, stay!

MERCHANTS [In chorus]
We take the Golden Road to Samarkand.

AN OLD MAN
Have you not girls and garlands in your homes?
Eunuchs and Syrian boys at your command?
Seek not excess: God hateth him who roams!

MERCHANTS [In chorus]
We take the Golden Road to Samarkand.

HASSAN
Sweet to ride forth at evening from the wells
When shadows pass gigantic on the sand,
And softly through the silence beat the bells
Along the Golden Road to Samarkand.

ISHAK
We travel not for trafficking alone;
By hotter winds our fiery hearts are fanned:
For lust of knowing what should not be known,
We take the Golden Road to Samarkand.

MASTER OF THE CARAVAN
Open the gate, O watchman of the night!

THE WATCHMAN

Ho, travellers, I open. For what land
Leave you the dim-moon city of delight?

MERCHANTS [With a shout]
We take the Golden Road to Samarkand!

[The **CARAVAN** passes through the gate.

WATCHMAN [Consoling the **WOMEN**]
What would ye, ladies? It was ever thus.
Men are unwise and curiously planned.

A WOMAN
They have their dreams, and do not think of us.

[The **WATCHMAN** closes the gate.

VOICES OF THE CARAVAN [In the distance singing]
We take the Golden Road to Samarkand.

AN ESSAY ON JAMES LEROY FLECKER by JC SQUIRE

In person Flecker was tall, with blue eyes, black, straight hair, and dark complexion. There was a tinge of the East in his appearance, and his habitual expression was a curious blend of the sardonic and the gentle. Until illness incapacitated him he was physically quite active, but his principal amusement was conversation, of which he never tired. He felt acutely the loss of good talk during his years abroad, in Syria especially. He was sociable, and enjoyed meeting and talking with crowds of people; but he had few intimate friends at Oxford, and, after he left England, little opportunity of making any. One of the few, Mr. Frank Savery, now of the British Legation, Berne, sends the following notes:

"My acquaintance with him began in January 1901, when he was a lanky, precocious boy of sixteen, and lasted, with long interruptions, until his death. His fate took him to the Near East, mine took me to Germany: for this reason we never met from 1908 to 1914, though we never ceased to correspond. Largely because our intercourse was thus broken, I believe that I am better able to appreciate the changes which his character underwent in the latter years of his life than those who never lost sight of him for more than a few months at a time.

"It was at Oxford that I first came to know him intimately. He was extraordinarily undeveloped, even for an English Public School boy, when he first went up in 1902. He already wrote verses—with an appalling facility that for several years made me doubt his talent. He imitated with enthusiasm and without discrimination, and, the taste in those long-gone days being for Oscar Wilde's early verse and Swinburne's complacent swing, he turned out a good deal of decadent stuff, that was, I am convinced, not much better than the rubbish written by the rest of his generation at Oxford. What interested me in Flecker in those days was the strange contrast between the man—or rather the boy—and his work. Cultured Oxford in general, I should add, was not very productive at that time: a sonnet a month was about the maximum output of the lights of Balliol. The general style of literature in favour at the time did not lend itself to a generous outpouring. Hence there was a certain piquancy in the exuberant flow of passionate verse which issued from Flecker's ever-ready pen in spite of his entire innocence of any experience whatever.

"Furthermore, he was a wit—a great wit, I used to think, but no humorist—and, like most wits, he was combative.

He talked best when some one baited him. At last it got to be quite the fashion in Oxford to ask Flecker to luncheon and dinner-parties—simply in order to talk. The sport he afforded was usually excellent.... Looking back on it now, I believe I was right in thinking that in those days he had no humour (there is very little humour in Oxford); nor am I so entirely sure that his wit was bad. I had, at any rate, a growing feeling that, in spite of his immaturity and occasional bad taste, he was the most important of any of us: his immense productiveness was, I vaguely but rightly felt, better and more valuable than our finicky and sterile good taste.

"By 1906 he had developed greatly—largely thanks to the companionship of an Oxford friend whom, in spite of long absence and occasional estrangements, he loved deeply till the end of his life. Even his decadent poems had improved: poor as are most of the poems in 'The Bridge of Fire,' they are almost all above the level of Oxford poetry, and there are occasional verses which forecast some of his mature work. Thus I still think that the title-poem itself is a rather remarkable achievement for a young man and not without a certain largeness of vision. The mention of this poem reminds me of an episode which well illustrates the light-heartedness which at that time distinguished the self-styled 'lean and swarthy poet of despair.' I was sitting with him and another friend in his rooms one day—early in 1906, I think—when he announced that he was going to publish a volume of poems. 'What shall I call it?' he asked. We had made many suggestions, mostly pointless, and almost all, I have no doubt, indecent, when Flecker suddenly exclaimed: 'I'll call it "The Bridge of Fire," and I'll write a poem with that name and put it in the middle of the book instead of the beginning. That'll be original and symbolic too.' We then debated the not unimportant question of what 'The Bridge of Fire' would be about. At midnight we parted, the question still unsettled. Flecker, however, remarked cheerfully that it did not much matter—it was a jolly good title and he'd easily be able to think of a poem to suit it.

"Flecker always cherished a great love for Oxford: he had loved it as an undergraduate, and afterwards not even the magic of the Greek seas, deeply as he felt it, ever made him forget his first university town. But on the whole I think that Cambridge, where he went to study Oriental languages in preparation for his consular career, did more for him. I only visited him once there—in November 1908, I think—but I had the distinct impression that he was more independent than he had been at Oxford. He was writing the first long version—that is to say, the third actual draft—of the 'King of Alsander.' Incidentally he had spoilt the tale, for the time being, by introducing a preposterous sentimental conclusion, a departure to unknown lands, if I remember rightly, with the peasant-maid, who had not yet been deposed, as she was later on, from her original position of heroine.

"And now follow the years in which my knowledge of Flecker is drawn only from a desultory correspondence. I should like to quote from some of the letters he wrote me, but, alas, they are in Munich with all my books and papers. He wrote to me at length whenever he had a big literary work on hand; otherwise an occasional post card sufficed, for he was a man who never put either news or gossip into his letters. I knew of his marriage; I knew that his literary judgment, as expressed in his letters and exemplified in his writings, had improved suddenly and phenomenally. That was all.

"At last his health finally collapsed and he came to Switzerland. It was at Locarno, in May 1914, that I saw him again. He was very ill, coughed continually, and did not, I think, ever go out during the whole fortnight I spent with him. He had matured even more than I had expected....

"He was very cheerful that spring at Locarno—cheerful, not extravagantly optimistic, as is the way of consumptives. I think he hardly ever mentioned his illness to me, and there was certainly at that time nothing querulous about him. His judgment was very sound, not only on bocks but also on men. He confessed that he had not greatly liked the East—always excepting, of course, Greece—and that his intercourse with Mohammedans had led him to find more good in Christianity than he had previously suspected. I gathered that he had liked his work as Consul, and he once said to me that he was very proud of having been a good businesslike official, thereby disposing, in his case at any rate, the time-honoured conception of the poet as an unpractical dreamer. He was certainly no mere dreamer at any period of his life; he appreciated beauty with extraordinary keenness, but, like a true poet, he was never contented with mere appreciation. He was determined to make his vision as clear to others as it was to himself.

"I saw Flecker once more, in December 1914. He was already visibly dying, and at times growing weakness numbed his faculties. But he was determined to do two things—to complete his poem, 'The Burial in England,' and to put his business affairs into the hands of a competent literary agent. The letters and memoranda on the latter subject which he dictated to me were admirably lucid, and I remember that, when I came to read them through afterwards, I found there was hardly a word which needed changing.

"One evening he went through the 'Burial' line byline with Mrs. Flecker and myself. He had always relied greatly on his wife's taste, and I may state with absolute certainty that the only two persons who ever really influenced him in literary matters were the Oxford friend I have already mentioned and the lady whose devotion prolonged his life, and whose acute feeling for literature helped to a great extent to confirm him in his lofty ideals of artistic perfection.

"Although he never really finished the longer version of the 'Burial' which he had projected, the alterations and additions he made that evening—'Toledo-wrought neither to break nor bend ' was one of the latter—were in the mam improvements and in no way suggested that his end was so near. To me, of course, that poem must always remain intolerably sad, but, as I re-read it the other day, I asked myself whether the casual reader would feel any trace of the 'mattrass grave' on which it was written. Candidly I do not think that even the sharpest of critics would have known, if he had not been told, that half the lines were written within a month of the author's death."

His letters, as is remarked above, were generally business-like and blunt. I have found a few to myself: they are almost all about his work, with here and there a short, exclamatory eulogy of some other writer. He observes, in December 1913, that a journal which had often published him had given "The Golden Journey" "an insolent ten-line review with a batch of nincompoops"; then alternately he is better and writing copiously, or very ill and not capable of a word. In one letter he talks of writing on Balkan Politics and Italy in Albania; in another of translating some war-poetry of Paul Deroulede's.

Another time he is even thinking of "having a bang at the Cambridge Local Examination... with a whack in it at B. Shaw." Then in November 1914 he says: "I have exhausted myself writing heroic great war-poems." He might comprehensibly have been in low spirits, dying there in a dismal and deserted "health resort " among the Swiss mountains, with a continent of war-zones cutting him off from all chance of seeing friends. But he always wrote cheerfully, even when desperately ill. The French recovery filled him with enthusiasm; he watched the Near Eastern tangle with the peculiar interest of one who 'knew the peoples involved; and in one delicate and capricious piece of prose, published in a weekly in October, he recalled his own experiences of warfare. He had had glimpses of the Turco-Italian War: Italian shells over Beyrout ("Unforgettable the thunder of the guns shaking the golden blue of sky and sea while not a breath stirred the palm-trees, not a cloud moved on the swanlike snows of Lebanon") and a "scrap" with the Druses, and the smoke and distant rumble of the battle of Lemnos, "the one effort of the Turks to secure the mastery of the Ægean." These were his exciting memories:

"To think that it was with cheerful anecdotes like these that I had hoped, a white-haired elder, to impress my grandchildren! Now there's not a peasant from Picardy to Tobolsk but will cap me with tales of real and frightful tragedy. What a race of deep-eyed and thoughtful men we shall have in Europe now that all those millions have been baptized in fire!"

Then in the first week of January 1915 he died. I cannot help remembering that I first heard the news over the telephone, and that the voice which spoke was Rupert Brooke's.

J. C. SQUIRE

James Elroy Flecker – A Short Biography

James Elroy Flecker was born on 5th November 1884, in Lewisham, London to father William Hermann Flecker, an Anglican clergyman and mother Sarah (née Ducat) both of Polish Jewish origin. Both had fled to England because of persecution when they converted to Christianity.

Flecker was baptized as Herman Elroy Flecker, but later chose to use "James". He was educated at Dean Close School, Cheltenham, where his father was the headmaster, and then Uppingham School before proceeding to Trinity College, Oxford, and Gonville and Caius College, Cambridge. While at Oxford he was greatly influenced by the last years of the Aesthetic movement there under John Addington Symonds, and became a close friend of the classicist and art historian John Beazley.

At this stage Flecker does not seem to have been greatly motivated by academic study. He only achieved third-class honours in Greats in 1906. This did not set him up for a job in either government service or the academic world.

After some frustrating forays at school teaching in 1907 he attempted to enter the Levant Consular Service, more properly known as "His Majesty's Consular service in the Ottoman dominions, Persia, Greece and Morocco". The job came with a salary of £200 per annum. However, if after two years the entrant failed the examinations his bond of £500 (mainly provided by his parents) would be lost. On the positive side the standard of entrants was generally rather low as the jobs outcome was not in the exotic European and world capitals but unattractive climates or dreary oriental provincial towns.

Preparations for the Student Interpreters' examination involved two years' study at Cambridge, learning the local languages. As we know academic study was not a motivator for Flecker and the first of these two years was at best far below what he could do. He was placed 4th out of 6 candidates, with the "clever but erratic" phrase marked on his file. Now knowing that all might now be lost Flecker realised that his primary ambition of a literary and poetic career was far from being certain and a back-up plan of a secure job had to be made safe. He duly knuckled down and passed the consular examinations with first-class honours. It was now reported to the Home Office that "Mr. Flecker has recovered the ground he lost last year in a really marvellous way and deserves the highest credit for the way he has worked during the last year".

He now entered the Levant Consular Service and in June 1910 was dispatched to the Ottoman capital of Constantinople, where he was attached to the British consulate.

However, Flecker's poetry career had made progress and he was beginning to garner praise for his poetry volumes including "The Bridge of Fire" from 1907 and "The Last Generation", a short novel in 1908. Works would now follow on a regular basis. He worked slowly but with great precision and paid far more attention to his writing than his job. Unfortunately, the then dreaded tuberculosis was also making progress in him. The preliminary symptoms were already apparent, and bouts of ill health were to alternate with periods of physical well-being woven with mental euphoria and creativity. He had already spent a period in back in England in the Cotswolds convalescing at a sanitorium. These episodes would now be a feature of his life.

On the boat to Constantinople, he fell in love with a Greek woman from Athens, Hellt Skiaderessi, and married her, in the face of parental anxiety about his lowly salary and his future health prospects, in May 1911.

He seems to have performed his consular duties, when he was well, in Constantinople, Smyrna and then, after September 1911, as Vice-Consul in Beirut, in a careless and rather sloppy manner. He and Hellt were always stretched financially and required frequent subsidies from home.

His continuing examinations in Ottoman Law were not properly prepared for. Some were failed and once he was very nearly dismissed, putting the £500 bond once more in danger of being forfeited. For unknown reasons the Foreign Office in London were tolerant over this putting it down to his ongoing battle with tuberculosis and tolerant of his extended periods of leave.

Flecker began work on "Hassan" during a stay on Corfu in the summer of 1911 where he was working on his Turkish for a forthcoming consular examination and was reading various works in Turkish, including a volume of farcical tales, in one of which a simple old man, Hassan, is duped over a supposed love philtre by a Jewish magician, Zachariah. Flecker set his rendition in Baghdad rather than Turkey and began work.

Hassan too was much revised, and the final version, which was to form the basis for the acting text—Flecker was adamant that it should appear on the London stage—was not made till Autumn 1914 when he was at Davos. During its three-year gestation it went from a play with pantomime elements to a drama of human disillusionment and a climax of high tragedy. (Sadly, with the brutal intervention of World War I and the need for elaborate and expensive staging it would not debut on a London Stage until 20th September 1923, although it had premiered three months earlier in a German translation in Darmstadt.)

A visit to Damascus for Christmas 1911, a city he was always enchanted by, provided inspiration for "The Gates of Damascus", a poem it is said "marks the high point of Flecker's achievement in the oriental mood, since it combines powerful and concentrated ideas with an assured and free manipulation of the

Persian-style internal and external rhymes". Flecker would also describe this as his greatest poem. In 1913 he had written a friend saying "I consider this to be my greatest poem ... It was inspired by Damascus itself by the way. I loathe the East and the Easterns, and spent all my time there dreaming of Oxford. Yet it seems, even to hardened Orientalists, that I understand".

Much of Flecker's work was based on Islamic themes and is immensely satisfying. However, Flecker himself seems to be at growing odds with them in reality often demonstrating an increasing lack of sympathy and respect to them.

As Flecker's health continued to deteriorate he now spent the last twenty months of his life in sanitoriums in Leysin and Davos. Here he carefully revised and improved all his work, usually producing more disciplined and pleasing versions of his works.

James Elroy Flecker died on 3rd January 1915, of tuberculosis, in Davos, Switzerland. His death at the age of thirty was described at the time as "unquestionably the greatest premature loss that English literature has suffered since the death of Keats".

James Elroy Flecker – A Concise Bibliography

Poetry
The Bridge of Fire (1907)
Thirty-Six Poems (1910)
Forty-Two Poems (1911)
The Golden Journey to Samarkand (1913)
The Old Ships (1915)
The Collected Poems (1916)

Novels
The Last Generation: A Story of the Future (1908)
The King of Alsander (1914)

Drama
Hassan: The Story of Hassan of Baghdad & How he Came to Make the Golden Journey to Samarkand (1922)
Incidental music to the play was written by Frederick Delius in 1920, before the play's publication, and first performed in September 1923.
Don Juan (1925)

Other
The Grecians (1910)
The Scholars' Italian Book (1911)
Collected Prose (1920)
The Letters of J.E. Flecker to Frank Savery (1926)
Some Letters from Abroad of James Elroy Flecker (1930)

Printed in Great Britain
by Amazon